The Fourth

COTSWOLD RAMBLES

23 short walks in the finest
part of the Cotswolds

Harry Hargreaves

Note: All these rambles are different
from those in Cotswold Rambles Books 1, 2&3

Cover photograph:
On the way to Haresfield Topograph (Ramble 2)

Published by
Thornhill Press
24 Moorend Road
Cheltenham

THORNHILL PRESS
MCMXCI

ISBN 0 946328 29 3

Typesetting by Wyvern Typesetting, Worcester
Printed by Billing & Sons Ltd., Worcester.

AUTHORS' NOTE

Months of more weekly wandering in the Cotswolds have resulted in the discovery of many walks which are not in our other three books of Cotswold Rambles but are of equal merit, charm and interest. The walks in this fourth book have been included only after the rejection of some we feel did not come up to the standard required. We therefore feel confident that walkers will find this book as good as, perhaps even better than, any of the other three.

We wish to thank those who have made the descriptions easier by signposting and waymarking and those farmers and landowners who have cooperated in keeping open rights of way. We have appreciated especially the signs on footpaths which say responsible walkers are welcomed by landowners.

Our thanks also go to those who have made such kindly, encouraging comments.

Richard Burlingham
Fred Evans
Harry Hargreaves
Fred Heathfield
David Hughes
Max Lovatt
Tony Lyon
Herbert Watts

A thumb-nail sketch of the author and his companions

Richard Burlingham — A retired Agricultural Merchant whose colourful leg ware and a detestation of split infinitives bring an added 'je ne sais quoi' to our otherwise harmless exertions.

Fred Evans — An ancient mariner with an addiction to both oat cuisine and—to quote John Speed—that bastard kind of wine called perry.

Harry Hargreaves — An even more ancient mariner and undisputed leader of the pack, with a penchant for white shorts in summer heatwaves, and with a wife who provides sustenance and first class chocolate cake. Is he, at age 91, the oldest practising Rambler and Author?

Fred Heathfield — A near professional cartographer and erstwhile schoolmaster whose recollections of life as a POW keep us enthralled.

David Hughes — A retired Bank Manager whose bearded features belie an encyclopaedic knowledge of the back streets of Birmingham where he brings comfort to aged bank employees.

Max Lovatt — Another retired Bank Manager whose exploits on the Dutch walking circuit, whose appetite for 'faggots-au-Nimpsfield' and his sartorial elegance are a never ending source of wonder to his companions.

Tony Lyon — The rookie of our group—once a schoolmaster. Alone wedded to metrication and with the remainder of the ensemble dedicated to early starts, pursues the opening stages of all walks in a somnambulent state—his dog leading.

Herbert Watts — A surveyor of yore whose knowledge of the outside and inside of more pubs than most of us have had hot dinners, keeps us on our architectural toes and adds that little bit of tone and serious purpose to our walks.

The aggregate of the ages of the above is exactly 600 years at the time of publication.

INTRODUCTION

Most of this introduction will be the same in substance as that in the third book but is so important it must be repeated.

This book contains over 120 miles of rambling. Some of it is on or related to well-used rights of way and near to popular places; other parts are remote and infrequently used and robust in character. Although described as short walks this does not mean they are all easy; they are not gentle strolls but require careful thought and concentration.

The narrative of each ramble is so detailed that it is hoped they can be followed without a map. But a map is desirable as sometimes there is a difficulty because of an alteration of the way (e.g. the diversion of a footpath, the taking up of a fence or the erection of a building which has taken place after the writing of the narrative). A map is also desirable as a means of recovery if the rambler makes a mistake in following the narrative. At the beginning of each ramble the number of the Ordnance Survey Map covering the area is stated and we recommend that these should be used. The printed map at the beginning of each ramble gives an outline of the way and can be followed with the narrative. If the rambler departs from the narrative through some interest or lack of concentration, the map should enable him to get back to the correct point. As in the third book, these maps have been produced by Mr. Fred Heathfield to whom again we wish to express our thanks.

It is stating the obvious to say: make sure you get to the right starting point; otherwise everything is wrong.

Whilst the Cotswolds do not have the dangers of mountains or wild moorlands some precautions will ensure that enjoyment is not marred. Therefore make sure your clothing and especially your footwear, are comfortable and adequate.

Allow at least one hour for each 2 miles of rambling. If you are an inexperienced walker allow much more. Make sure you have sufficient time to complete the ramble before sunset.

The numbers of the rambles on the sketch on the back cover indicate the areas from which the rambles begin.

Signs: Cotswold Way (CW), white dot on either yellow or blue arrow: Yellow arrow—footpath: Blue arrow—bridleway.

Whilst every endeavour has been made to ensure that each ramble follows throughout its length the existing Rights of Way (unless acknowledgement is made of special permission from the landowner) and care has been taken to ensure the accuracy of all information in the book, the Authors and Publisher cannot accept any liability for the accuracy of the information given or for its interpretation by readers.

THE COUNTRY CODE

Please remember as you walk throughout the countryside to respect the privacy and livelihood of those who live in the country. The Country Code asks you to:-

1. Guard against all risk of fire.
2. Fasten all gates.
3. Keep dogs under proper control.
4. Keep to paths across farmland.
5. Avoid damaging fences, hedges and walls.
6. Leave no litter.
7. Safeguard water supplies.
8. Protect wildlife, plants and trees.
9. Go carefully on country roads.
10. Respect the life of the countryside.

CONTENTS

Ramble 1, Daneway canal tunnel

Ramble 1

DANEWAY BRIDGE, TUNLEY HOUSE, WATERLANE

This is an interesting area with the Thames and Severn Canal running alongside the River Frome. The canal has a tunnel two miles long and was used between 1789 and 1911. The boats were propelled through the tunnel by the bargees lying on their backs and pushing with their feet against the roof of the tunnel. The Daneway Bridge Inn was built for the refreshment of the bargees and is near one of the forty locks which raised the canal to the level of the tunnel entrance.

Distance: 5 miles.

Maps: O.S. 163 in the 1:50 000 series. Sheet SO 80/90 in the 1:25 000 Pathfinder series.

Starting Point: Grid Reference 939 034 Daneway Bridge Inn.

To get to the starting point from Cirencester take the A419 road for about 4 miles and then take the right fork to Daneway Bridge.

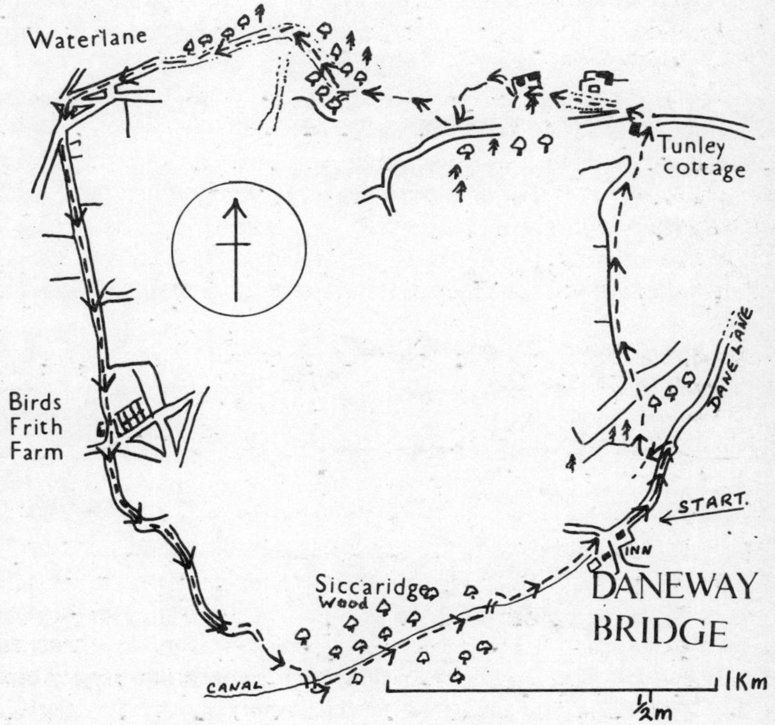

Leaving the Daneway Bridge Inn, turn right, up the road signposted to Miserden and, in about 300 yards cross the stile on the left at the footpath sign. Turn sharply left for a few yards, then the path curves to the right to two stiles, one on the left going back towards the inn and the other, a few yards to the right, leading up the hill. Take the stile on the right and follow the path up to the ridge and through a gap in the line of trees. Here there is a cross track but, directly ahead, is a gate in the angle of a broken wall. Pass through this gate into a very large field and walk ahead keeping close to the hedge on the left.

In about 400 yards this hedge curves away from the right of way, which is in a straight line ahead to the far point of the curve, but it may be better to stay close to the hedge, walking on the broad headland.

At the end of this curve the hedge turns away sharply to the left, but the path continues ahead to pass down the right hand side of Tunley Cottage, a house now restored and enlarged. Here the path meets the lane. Turn left on the lane and, in about 50 yards, take the right fork to Tunley House. This lane is now waymarked. Tunley House Farm is being extensively altered but the path turns in between the buildings to turn left behind the house. The path is waymarked with white plastic discs fixed to trees. Follow the marks down the valley towards a power line post which is also waymarked. Continue on down-hill, crossing a small stream and pass through a wicket gate into the wood.

Follow the path to cross two small streams, the first having a new bridge with hand-rail and the second with a simple plank bridge. Immediately turn right to follow the stream. The path is narrow but widens as another path comes in at a sharp angle from the left. The path climbs slightly away from the stream and passes a small gate in front of which a bridle path sign is set on a low post.

The path moves back towards the stream and, where a small flat bridge crosses the water from the right, turn sharply left, without crossing the stream, and follow the path uphill. Watercombe House comes into view on the right. In 200 yards the path ends at a gate with a stile at the side. Cross the stile and walk up the lane between the cottages to the road.

At the road junction cross straight over, following the sign for Oakridge and Lynch. In 100 yards, at a sign post, diverge left away from the road along a green lane which runs in a straight line for about ½ mile to the cross roads at Birds Frith Farm.

Cross over and take the lane ahead which, after about 200 yards, curves down past Iles's House, whose gardens and grounds have a spectacular display of daffodils and snowdrops in the Spring. Beyond the house take the right fork downhill marked 'Unsuitable for Motors', and continue to Trillis Cottage. The road deteriorates into a rough track, which crosses a small stream, and continues towards a bridge over the remains of the Thames and Severn Canal.

Cross over the bridge and turn left to walk along the canal bank on the Sapperton Wood side. The River Frome is quite close on the right hand side. The path crosses to the other bank of the canal and passes several Lock chambers. Keeping the canal now on the right continue to Daneway Bridge and the end of the walk.

Ramble 2, Haresfield Topograph

Ramble 2

EDGE, HARESFIELD BEACON, STANDISH WOOD

A walk with many interesting features and excellent views.

Distance: 7½ miles.

Maps: OS 162 Gloucester and the Forest of Dean in the 1:50 000 series and SO 80/90 in the Pathfinder 1:25 000 series.

Starting Point: Grid reference 847 098, 250 yards south of Edge church on the Edge to Whiteshill and Randwick road at the stone shelter.

To get to Edge: From Gloucester take the A4173 south for 5 miles. From Painswick take the first road on the right going west, immediately south of the church, for 1 mile.

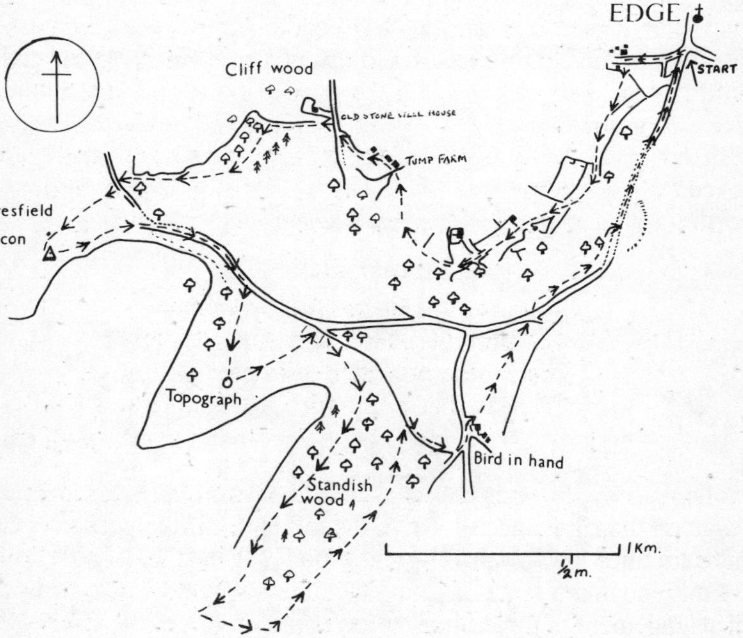

Take the minor road, directly opposite the shelter, signposted 'Harescombe, gradient 1 in 6' and, in 300 yards, take the footpath on the left opposite Hill House Farm crossing the stile by the bungalow. The path is narrow with a hedge on the left and a barbed wire fence on the right. In fifty yards cross a second stile into an open field and bear left to the far corner by the wood where a waymarked stile by the gate gives access to the wood. In about sixty yards leave the wood by a waymarked stile and cross the field on the higher side, alongside the wood which is on your left, to the corner by the trees where there is another waymarked stile on the right of a gate adjacent to the ruins of a stone building.

Cross the stile and turn right onto a tarmac track dropping downhill to Randall's Farm. The gate has a Private notice but the footpath is a right of way and is followed to the point where it turns sharply to the right and down to the farm-house but here take the stile on the left by the trees. Keep the trees on the left for about 100 yards to the corner of the field and cross another waymarked stile. Go ahead over 2 more waymarked stiles. In the next field the path appears to rise towards the wood but ignore this and bear right to pass between two large mounds and then through a metal gate. Continue alongside the buildings of Tump Farm. At the end of the buildings on your right, turn left to a metal gate and stile which gives access to a farm lane. (This rises to the road at Cliffwell Cottages.)

Turn right and in a few yards left along a track signposted Haresfield Beacon. At the beginning of this track is the old stone well house. It is worth looking into this; it has an inscription reading:

'Deo Gratias

Whoever the bucket full upwindeth
Let him bless God who water findeth
Water here but small availeth
Go seek that well which never faileth.'

John Ch.4 v.14

The path by the well house rises in rough, broad steps with a beech hedge on the right and woods on the left and, through gaps on the right there are fine views towards Robins Wood Hill and the City of Gloucester.

Continue in the same direction to a point where the path turns left and an arrangement of three large stones commemorates the Civil War seige of Gloucester. In a further 600 or 700 yards the path meets the road at Ring Hill Farm. Turn left for 30 yards then right at the waymark for Haresfield Beacon. You are now on the Cotswold Way. The path rises to the waymarked stile which gives access to the open area around the Beacon, and the trig point. Follow the way indicated by the waymark to the trig point.

From the trig point turn sharply back in a north easterly direction following a well defined path round the contour for about 200 yards to a waymarked stile. Go over the stile and follow the path from which Gloucester and its Cathedral can be seen away on the left. Follow the edge to another waymarked stile and a gate in a wall. In another 120 yards the path emerges onto a road. Here a path on the right marked Cotswold Way clearly leads to the Topograph. Do not take this unless you wish to make a steep descent and ascent. Instead, walk on or by the road for about 400 yards to a very narrow squeeze stile in the wall on the right which is signposted Randwick 2 Km and which gives access to an open area. (The squeeze stile is shown on the front cover.)

From here go directly south, passing to the right of a small cluster of trees. The Topograph will soon be seen and go directly to it. On leaving the Topograph, turn back at an angle of about 45 degrees east, passing to the left of a clump of trees to rejoin the road recently left at a car park. Turn right on the road and immediately go through the gate into Standish Wood, taking the extreme right of several tracks. The path is well defined and is followed for about a mile to where it rises to a barrier with a low stile on the right. Shortly after the barrier at a clearly defined cross track, turn left uphill to a much broader track with various waymarks.

Turn left and follow the Cotswold Way signs along this bridle track for about 400 yards. Here leave the bridle path by taking a footpath on the left which is a continuance of the Cotswold Way as is indicated by a mark on a stone slab. Follow the Cotswold Way signs for about ¾ mile and at a junction of 5 tracks, leave the Cotswold Way by going straight ahead.

In about 70 yards, at a stone wall, pass through a squeeze stile into an open field and turn right. Go ahead with the wood on your right to the road. Turn left and, in a few yards, meet the road into Whiteshill. Bear left, ignore the waymark by the post box named Bird in Hand, and continue on the road for about 100 yards to where a waymark on the right, and immediately beyond a house, shows the way across an open field. Cross diagonally left towards the far corner to a stile and out and across the road into the wood by a wooden stile. Almost immediately turn right on a clear path, which follow for about 400 yards through the trees until it emerges onto the Edge road opposite some old quarries. Turn left on the road and go ahead for about ½ mile back to the start of the walk.

WOODCHESTER, SELSLEY COMMON

A pleasant country walk with impressive high level views from Selsey Common.

Distance: 4 miles.

Maps: OS 162 in the 1:50 000 series and SO 80/90 Stroud in the Pathfinder 1:25 000 series.

Starting Point: Grid reference 839 026 near Woodchester village church.

To get to Woodchester from Stroud take the A46 southwards for about 1½ miles; then take the signposted road on the right to Woodchester.

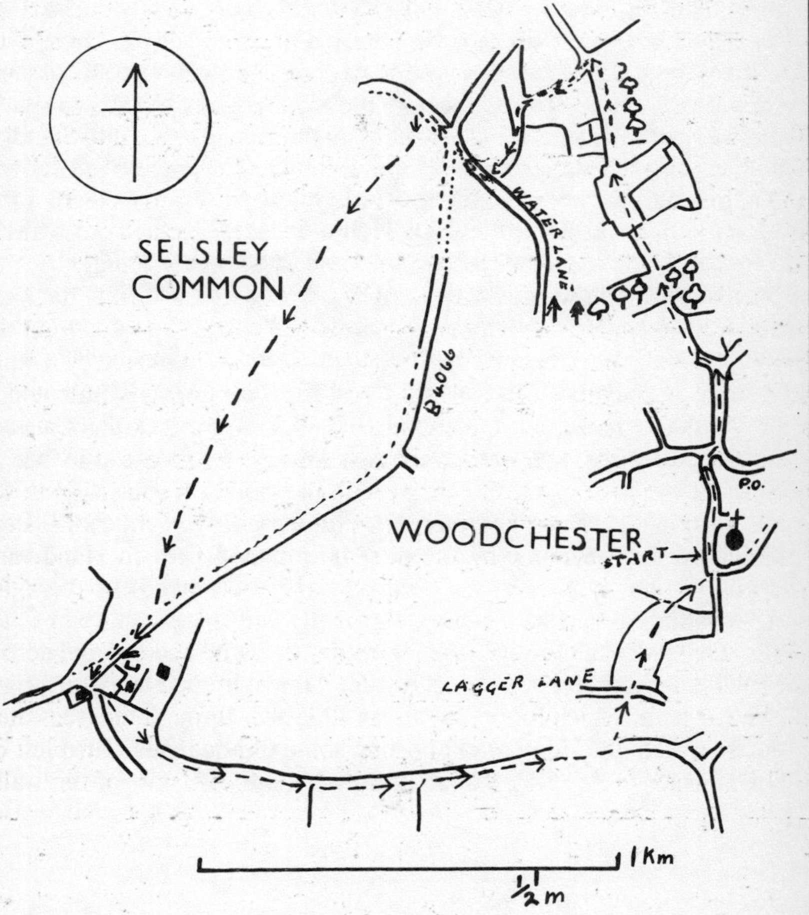

With the church on the right follow the minor road northwards to the main road. Turn right for a short distance then take the minor road first left. Follow it for 200 yards and at a sharp right bend locate and proceed along a waymarked footpath on the left. Pass through a kissing gate into pasture and continue across the field with a boundary wall on the right to a waymarked stile. Cross and ascend the narrow track through a strip of woodland and cross a waymarked stile into further pasture. Leave the field over a waymarked stile and then immediately over another stile into more pasture. Follow the path ahead across the field, go over a waymarked stile and continue on a well defined track between light woodland.

At a cross track just before farm buildings, go left over a stile into a field. Proceed across the field alongside the boundary hedge on the right to pass over another stile on to an unsurfaced service road. Turn left—southwards—and at the end, opposite a house, go right and pass through an opening in the boundary fence giving access to a pasture field. Cross the field with a hedge on the left and leave via a double stile on to a surfaced lane—Water Lane. Turn right, ascend to and cross over main road and continue ahead to the brow of the hill. Here, take the definite track on the left leading to Selsley Common.

Proceed ahead to a fork and take the right hand fork to follow the wide track in a south westerly direction. At the second fork take the right hand green hollow track. Fine views of the Stroud district can be seen on the right. Continue over Selsley Common at a high level for about ½ mile, gradually bearing left. Straight ahead in the distance a house will be seen which is on the road; make slightly to the right of this. A cluster of farm buildings will come into view. Walk directly towards these and continue to the road.

Turn right at the road for a short distance and at the entrance to Brownhill Farm, where power lines cross the road, take the signposted path on the left. Cross a stile and proceed in the direction indicated. Continue ahead over pasture with Dingle Wood on the immediate left and follow the edge of the wood in an easterly direction for about ½ mile, crossing two waymarked stiles en route. Where the wood ends, cross a further waymarked stile on to a minor road and turn left.

Descend for about 50 yards to locate a signposted path on the left. Follow the path between houses; go over a signposted stile into pasture and walk in the direction indicated. Leave the field over a waymarked stile, pass over a small service road—Laggar Lane—then cross another waymarked stile. Continue ahead northwards over pasture, cross a further waymarked stile and descend to a stream. Pass over the stream on stone slabs, cross a waymarked stile and continue uphill towards

Woodchester church seen ahead. Leave the field through a kissing gate to the road near the church where the walk started.

Ramble 4, Bagendon Church

Ramble 4

WOODMANCOTE, BAGENDON, NORTH CERNEY, RIVER CHURN

A pleasant walk which includes two interesting villages each with a fine church.

Distance: 8 miles.

Maps: OS 163 in the 1:50 000 series and SP 00/10 and SO 80/90 in the 1:25 000 series.

Starting Point: Grid reference 004 091—village of Woodmancote.

To get to Woodmancote from Cirencester leave on the A417(T) going NW. In about 1 mile fork right along A435 to North Cerney. From there take a road on the left to Woodmancote.

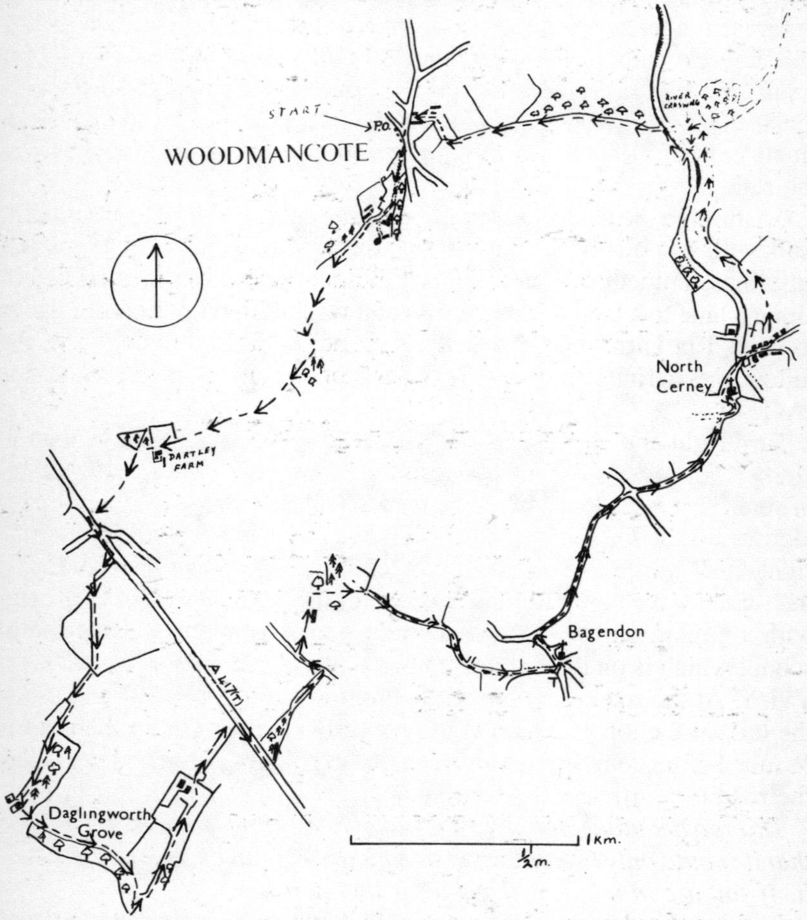

From the telephone kiosk in the centre of the village walk south for 30 yards to take a green track on the right. In a few yards at a metalled road veer left to continue in the same direction between a large house (Moorwood) and some farm buildings. In 200 yards bear left at track junction for about ¾ mile to Dartley Farm. Turn left and continue to main road.

Cross this very busy road with care, turn left and walk up verge past a road on the right which goes to Middle Duntisbourne. In about 150 yards past this road locate an indefinite path on the right which in 3 yards leads to a gate. Go through (or over) and walk ahead with a wall and hedge on the left. In 150 yards pass through a gate on the left and go ahead with the wall and a rough hedge now on the right (the hedge finishes but the wall continues) for about 300 yards to a facing gate. Go through and walk towards another gate seen ahead. Do not go through this gate but veer left and descend with a hedge on the right to the corner of the field and into a sunken lane. Just before a group of houses at the bottom of the lane, locate a waymarked hunting gate on the left. (The houses ahead are the small village of Duntisbourne Rouse with its charming little church on the right.)

Go through the gate and ascend a definite path; pass through a gate and walk with a wood on the right passing through another gate to some farm buildings. Immediately past the last building on the left, turn sharp left along a lane to a facing fence; cross and walk with wire fence on the left to High Tun Farm seen ahead. Pass round the farm buildings and then follow the definite track with a fence on the right to the main road (A417T).

Turn right and in 300 yards at the end of a wood on the left, turn left along a very definite track and continue to the road. Here turn left and in about 150 yards take a track on the right which descends to Oysterwell House. Just before the house bear left and pass the house which is on the right. In 30 yards take a descending track (which can be very muddy) on the right. At the bottom of the descent follow the track round to the right with a stream on the left and so walk into Bagendon. Passing the old school which is on the left one comes to the church which is well worth a visit. At the road junction just before the church turn left and ascend the hill, at the top of which at the memorial, turn right up the road for ½ mile before coming to a cross roads. Go straight ahead and walk down the road to North Cerney Church.

This is a beautiful church and is full of interesting features. It is so good that it should only be seen when adequate time can be devoted to viewing it. If you are in a hurry, leave it for another day.

Leaving the church on the right walk down to the main road: cross the road and walk past the Bathurst Arms uphill. About 20 yards before the road forks locate a track on the left; ascend to pass through a gate. Continue ahead over the field descending to the left hand corner to pass through a gate on the left and into the riverside meadow. Follow the course of the river for about 500 yards to a hunting gate, through a small spinney and thence to the estate road (which leads to Rendcomb College). Here turn left, cross the bridge to the main road. Note: the description underlined is not a right of way but it has been included by kind permission of the landowner. This permission may be withdrawn at any time and is given on the understanding that it does not create a right of way.

Walk up the road to the right for about 200 yards to locate a wicket gate on the left and ascend through the wood to pass into the field on the left via a hunting gate. Walk in the same direction with a wall and the wood on the right, through a farm gate into another field. Pass under power lines. In a further 130 yards go through a gate on the right into a field. Walk towards some barns seen ahead and locate a stile just before a house on the left. Cross and walk into Woodmancote.

Ramble 5, Painswick

Ramble 5

PAINSWICK, WORGAN'S FARM, WINKRIDGE HILL, HAMMOND'S FARM

An interesting walk about the village and the adjoining countryside.
Distance: 6 miles.
Maps: OS 162 in the 1:50 000 series and SO 80/90 in the 1:25 000 Pathfinder series.
Starting Point: Car park south of Painswick Church grid reference 866 095.

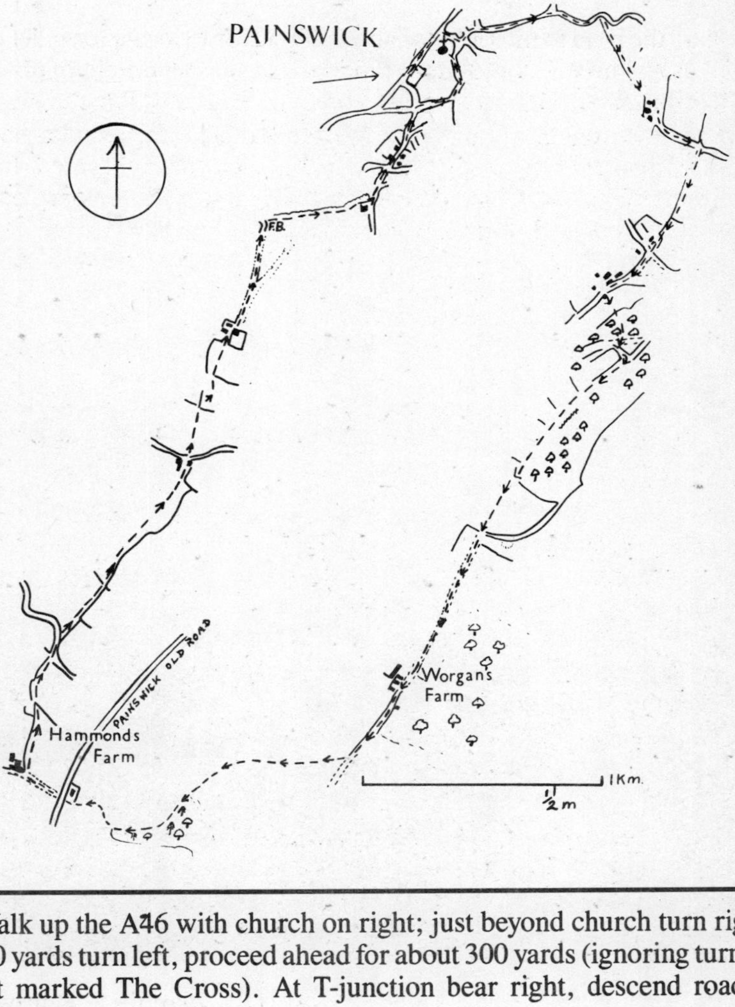

Walk up the A46 with church on right; just beyond church turn right. In 50 yards turn left, proceed ahead for about 300 yards (ignoring turning right marked The Cross). At T-junction bear right, descend road to where the road forks. Here take the right hand fork marked Sheepscombe.

In about 300 yards and just beyond Lovedays Mill locate a waymarked stile on the right. Cross, turn right and in 50 yards turn left uphill with hedgerow on the right (do not cross facing stile) to reach Dell Farm. Pass through farm and in about 300 yards turn right and follow line of hedge, keeping it on the left. At the field end cross stile, pass through wood gate, through farm and through a second gate to reach the road. Here turn left and at the road junction a few yards ahead turn right. In about 100 yards pass Greenhouse Court on the right; just beyond a junction of a road coming in from the left there are buildings on each side of the road. Just beyond these buildings a waymarked footpath crosses the road. Take the footpath to the left, cross stile, walk up field to another stile which leads into steeply ascending woodland.

Just after entering the wood a wide track is crossed and the footpath ascends steeply for about 200 yards to reach a second wide track (blue waymark on facing tree). Here turn left along this wide track and in about 50 yards turn right to arrive at a track junction in a clearing. Turn right on this bridleway and keep to the right hand track at a nearby junction, i.e. hold to the bridleway which runs along the hill crest. Along this section there is an open field on the right and woods on the left. On leaving the wood pass through a wooden hunting gate into a field with a wall on the right. Leave the field by a waymarked metal gate, go over cross track and walk straight on to Worgan's Farm seen ahead. There are some fine views of Stroud on the left.

About 300 yards after passing through Worgan's Farm take a waymarked footpath on the right. Where the track enters a wood bear left down the descending track and at a metalled road, marked Painswick Old Road on the map, cross and walk down to Hammonds Farm seen ahead. At the beginning of the buildings locate a double metal gate with waymarked stone stile alongside. Cross and hold hedge and then wall on the left to reach a waymarked stile in corner of the field. Cross this stile and continue with hedge on the left to a waymarked stile which gives egress on to a metalled road. Here turn left and descend for about 40 yards before taking a waymarked footpath on the right which leads to a stile. Cross this into the field and walk with hedge on the right. Pass through a metalled gate and over a facing stile into another field keeping the hedge on the right. A waymarked metal gate gives access to a track which passes between two cottages and then on to a metalled road.

Cross the road and pass over facing stile; hold direction across field. Climb fence at waymark and descend to a stream which cross by a wooden footbridge before ascending to a waymarked stile in the facing fence. At the house ahead, Sheephouse, locate and pass through waymarked kissing gate to the left of the garden wall. Now follow a good metalled road towards Painwick, seen clearly ahead, for about 200 yards before descending left down a waymarked path towards Kingsmill House. Cross stream and walk along track till a waymarked stone bridge over the sluice control is located on the right. Pass over a stile into the field with the stream on the left. At the end of this meadow a stile gives access through a private garden, then to a metal fence and thence through a waymarked gap and on to the road. Here turn left and walk up the road. In about 400 yards and 20 yards past a house called Howbeg, locate a green lane on the right. In 120 yards this leads to an iron gate with stile alongside. Pass through and walk up the road for about 200 yards. Opposite Fig Tree Cottage turn left up a narrow path which soon becomes a tarmac lane leading into the churchyard. Turn left past the church porch to the main road. Turn left for about 100 yards to the car park and the start of the walk.

Ramble 6

EDGEWORTH, KING'S FARM, DANEWAY

Distance: 4 miles.

Map: OS 163 in 1:50 000 series. SO 80/90 in 1:25 000 Pathfinder.

Starting Point: Edgeworth Church 947 060.

To reach Edgeworth leave A417(T) at Duntisbourne Leer turn (983 083). It may also be approached from B4070 (Birdlip—Stroud) road turning left at Fostons Ash P.H. and within 200 yards left again through Whiteway. The Church and Manor are found at the end of a steeply descending dead end road in the village. Ample car parking is available here.

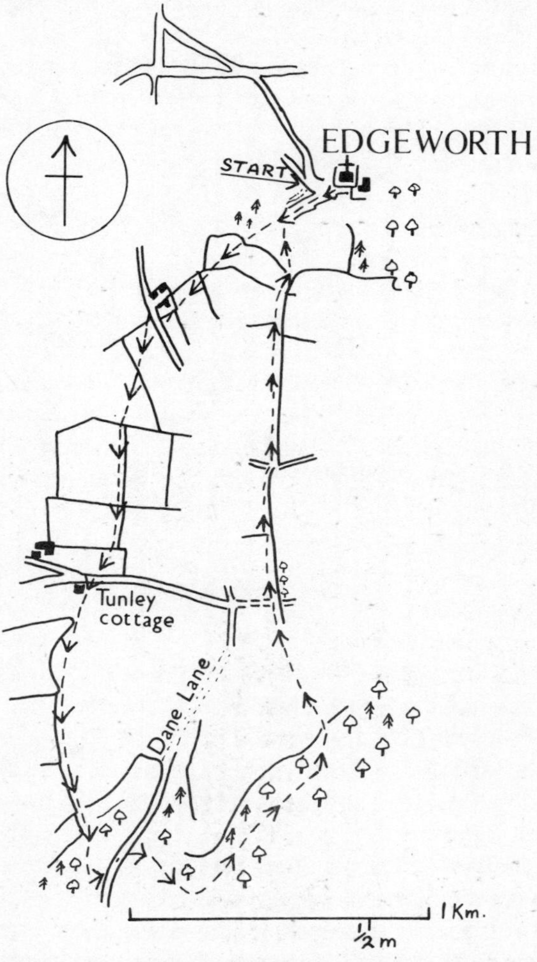

Standing with back to the Church and with the Manor on your left hand side, descend the facing metalled road. After some 400 yards, and beyond the last building on the right, pass through wood gate into pastureland. Maintain same direction passing waymarked tree stump and ascending to cross stile seen in fence ahead.

Proceed across field toward double set of metal gates (waymarked) and aim toward the left hand of two houses seen ahead (Field Barn). Locate and cross waymarked stile in facing fence and follow narrow path round paddock to reach road and waymark. Proceed directly across road and over stile and immediately bear half left across pastureland to cross firstly a stile over a wire fence and later a stile over a hedgerow. Cross track (with Kings Farm on your right) and proceed along field edge keeping wall and hedge on your left hand side.

At left hand corner of field boundary is located a stile. Cross and incline slightly right to reach gate leading from field. Once through gate head toward building seen ahead and crossing track to reach stile which gives access to road. Cross this road and ascend steps just left of building (Tunley Cottage) to enter field. Follow clear grass track between grassed sections and when hedge is reached, continue with hedge on your right hand side.

Where this hedge follows a right hand bow, the Right of Way continues in a straight line across the field. Since however there is a good headland, it may be more reasonable to follow this. The whole field section is about half a mile long and finishes at a gate in the wall. Once through this gate bear half left and cross grass track toward the hedgerow and, where ground descends steeply, turn half right and descend to stile seen below. Having crossed, turn half left for 20 yards to reach further stile. Cross and hold to descending grass track (ignoring gate and stile seen on right hand side) until road and waymarked post are reached. The road is Dane Lane. Daneway House* is seen across the road and Daneway with a P.H. lies a short distance down the road to the right. (Short diversion then possible to view the canal tunnel.)**

The route of this walk however crosses the road and follows an ascending track into the wood. This section can prove very muddy in wet conditions. Ignore the tracks—the results of logging operations—found some 50 yards, 150 yards and 250 yards respectively into the wood. Hold to the ascending track. In a further 200 yards, at next track fork, hold to ascending left hand track.

Approximately ¾ mile further is a cross track junction—here turn left and ascend moderately steeply, cross further track junction and in some 50 yards reach clearing at edge of wood. Here turn right to meet footpath enter field on left hand side. Follow good track along field edge (wall/hedge on right and open field on left) for some 500 yards until, at point where track becomes hedged on both sides, a stile and wood gate are located on right hand side.

Cross and follow good headland path through two fields holding hedge on right hand side. A cross track is met here (Gloucester Beeches) and a facing stile/gate. Cross and continue through two further fields (stiles positioned) and leave next field by way of a wooden gate and the last field by crossing the wooden horse jump found in the far right hand corner.

Once over, bear half left on descending grassland towards the left hand of the buidings seen. When reached, the track followed at the commencement of the walk has now been rejoined. Turn right, pass through wooden gate on to metalled road and continue until Edgeworth Manor and Church are again reached.

*Daneway House is a manor dating from 14th century. It was used for some twenty years by Ernest Gimson and the Barnsley brothers (followers of William Morris) as furniture workshops and showrooms.

**If the diversion to the Daneway P.H. is taken, one might well consider following the Right of Way which departs by a stile at the lower left of the P.H. car park (built on the site of the last canal lock before the tunnel). Once over, turn left, cross stile some 40 yards on and follow good towpath for about 500 yards with dried-up canal on left hand side. The north-west end of the 2 ¼ mile long tunnel on the Thames and Severn canal (linking the Stroudwater canal with the Thames) is viewed here. It should not be entered as it is blocked in two places. It was built in 1789—employing explosives for the first time in tunnel making—and was in use until 1928 when water loss closed it.

If this diversion is made, one must return past the P.H. and past Daneway House in order to rejoin the walk.

Ramble 7, Tyndale Monument

Ramble 7

WOTTON-under-EDGE, BRADLEY BARN, TYNDALE MONUMENT

A fine walk embracing strip lynchets (Celtic cultivation terraces), the Tyndale Monument and fine views over the Severn Valley.
Distance: 4½ miles.
Maps: OS 162 in 1:50 000 series. ST 69/79 in 1:25 000 Pathfinder series.
Starting Point: Grid reference 764 945, Bradley Barn on Old London Road.
Joining instructions as in walk no. 8.

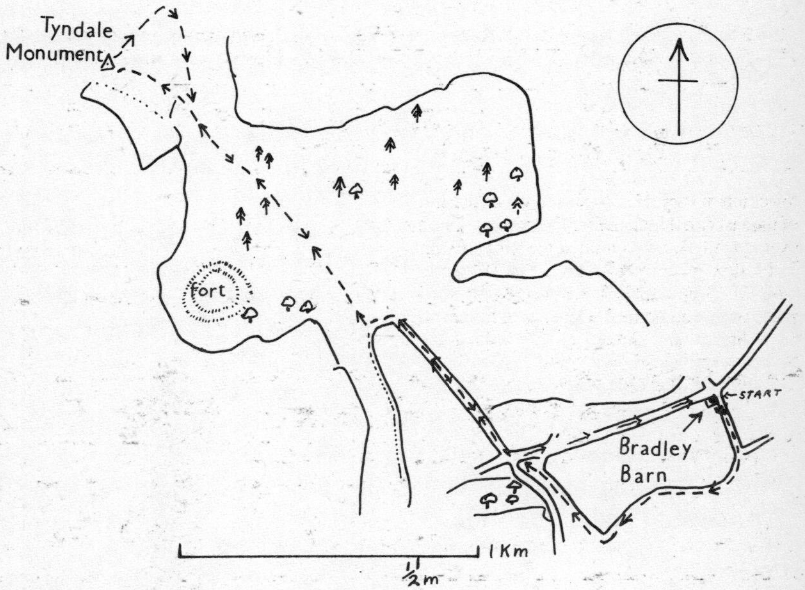

Facing Bradley Barn locate footpath sign to left of building. Follow this good track to a point where it turns left; here, locate and pass over waymarked stile ahead and bear right holding stone wall on immediate right. Follow broad grass track with lynchets visible below. This good track bears to the right and holds the contour and subsequently bears left with hedge on right hand side. Where hedge finishes, turn right and a grass topped reservoir is seen ahead. Skirt this, holding firstly reservoir and subsequently the wire fence on your right hand side and descend to reach track and trees ahead. Here turn right to reach stile and metal gate. Pass through gate; carry on up track to track junction; turn left and, in 200 yards, before ruined buildings, bear left along minor path to stile and road. (Signpost at stile—BW Coombe Hill.)

Turn left along road and in 20 yards turn right along a wide track (signpost BW Tyndale Monument). After some 600 yards, passing through a metal gate en route, a 5-track junction is reached. Here take the sharp left hand track and, in 100 yards, turn right, joining the Cotswold Way (CW). In 170 yards locate and follow a faint track on the right (painted waymark on tree); in another 150 yards, cross major track to another major track; cross this and walk along small track to a third major track; bear left and, almost immediately, go right to cross-tracks. Here, go straight ahead to stile, gate and large stone trough on right (CW marked) into pleasant beech coppice before debouching into open field with Tyndale Monument ahead.* Proceed to Monument and admire the excellent views of the Severn valley, Forest of Dean and—on a clear day—parts of South Wales.

With one's back to the iron kissing gate in the fence surrounding the monument, walk North East along the top of the ridge to CW marked stile on lower ground to the left and then into a wood.

In approximately 100 yards at a sunken track, turn right (at this point leaving the CW which goes downhill on the sunken track). Go over the stile in the wooden fence, along the track, through a metal gate and thence into the same field mentioned earlier and along the track to beech coppices and cross-tracks also mentioned earlier. Here take the right-hand track—CW marked—and follow these marks for ¾ mile. At the end of Westridge Wood (National Trust sign), take the left-hand track to the road (the right-hand track is marked CW).

Turn left along road and in ½ mile Bradley Barn is reached—the beginning and end of the walk.

*Tyndale Monument was erected in 1866 to commemorate the translator of the New Testament (together with the first five books of the Old Testament) into English. Tyndale was born locally, fled from England in 1525 and was subsequently imprisoned at Vilvorde (Belgium) and burnt at the stake in October 1563.

Ramble 8

WOTTON-under-EDGE, BRADLEY BARN, WATERLEY BOTTOM

A walk taking in the attractive Waterley Bottom.
Distance: 4 miles.
Map: OS 1262 in 1:50 000 series. ST 69/79 in 1:25 000 series.
Starting Point: Bradley Barn on Old London road. Grid reference 764 945.
To reach Bradley Barn from Wotton-under-Edge centre, follow B4058 north-east on ascending and winding road. In 1¼ miles take acute left hand turn and in a further 700 yards at marked cross tracks is Bradley Barn.

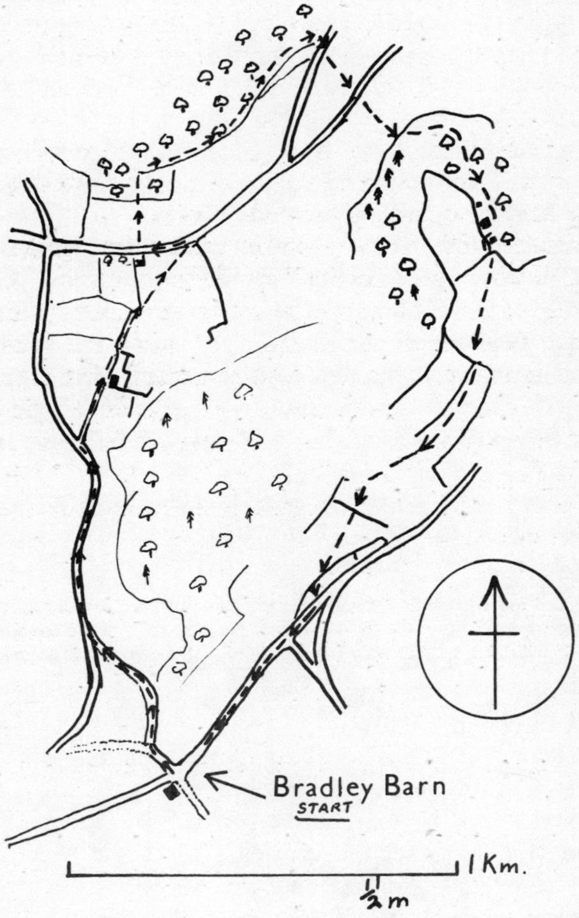

With the Bradley Barn buildings behind you, take the signposted bridleway downhill marked Spuncombe Bottom. At first fork (100 yards on with Woodland Trust sign facing) bear right and at next fork bear left to reach road in a further 400 yards.

Here turn right along road for 500 yards before taking waymarked footpath on right. In about 300 yards, and just short of Halfway Farm, cross stile in left hand hedge and walk due north with hedge on right; over another stile and in 100 yards locate a stile in hedge: cross and with hedge now on left proceed for 50 yards, then bear half right across field towards lone holly tree and beyond to reach waymarked stile and road. Looking left above the trees can be seen the top of the Tyndale Monument.

Turn left along road and in some 200 yards and opposite a farm building turn sharp right at sign post to an iron field gate. Pass through gate and immediately go left up field towards wood and large rough hedge. At a point in this hedge about 30 yards to the right of a large gap there is a track through the hedge: carry on to a waymarked stile at the beginning of the wood. Cross the stile and walk up stepped path for 86 steps to reach second break in flight and take right hand path (waymark on tree trunk here).

This path wanders through the wood for about 400 yards before emerging onto a broad track: turn acute right and in about 200 yards go down a track which comes in from the right: in 50 yards take the narrow sunken track which goes directly downhill past a house (Ridings View) on the left to reach the road.

Cross road; over stile and walk down the hill with hedge on left. Near the bottom of the slope, locate stile in left hand hedge: cross and walk diagonally right for 30 yards to another stile which gives access to a lane. Turn right and in 10 yards climb left hand bank to a V-stile. Walk up hill in a sunken lane between two hedges (this may be partly overgrown) to a stile and into Ridings Wood. The track through the wood winds upwards for about 200 yards before emerging onto a broad track. Here turn left for 15 yards and then take the right hand track leading up the hill for 150 yards before reaching a broad track: turn left and in about 160 yards look for a narrow track on the right which in about 50 yards emerges near a house and a large stone cross. Walk along the house drive to arrive at a cattle grid and open field.

Once in the field, walk slightly right of track aiming towards junction of rough hedge and trimmed shorter hedge seen ahead. Here is located a waymarked stile. Cross and turn left into field (again note good view of Tyndale Monument seen to your right on far hill).

Now turn right with wood on your right for 150 yards: veer slightly left to cross waymarked stile in facing hedge and walk on with hedge on right.

Where hedge turns sharp right carry straight on to stile in facing hedge. Cross and walk on with hedge on right to corner of field, through gap in hedge to next field: turn half left to waymarked stile in hedge and thence to road (finger post 'The Ridings'). Turn right on road and in about 700 yards Bradley Barn and the start of the walk will be reached.

Ramble 9

COLN VALLEY

A beautiful stretch of country in the winding valley of the River Coln.
Distance: 6 miles.
Maps: OS 163 in the 1:50 000 series. Sheet SP 00/10 in the 1:25 000 Pathfinder series.
Starting Point: Bridge over River Coln near Winson Mill Farm. Grid reference 088 090.
To get to Starting Point from Northleach go SW along A429 to Fosbridge, then through Coln St. Denis to Coln Roger to Winson.

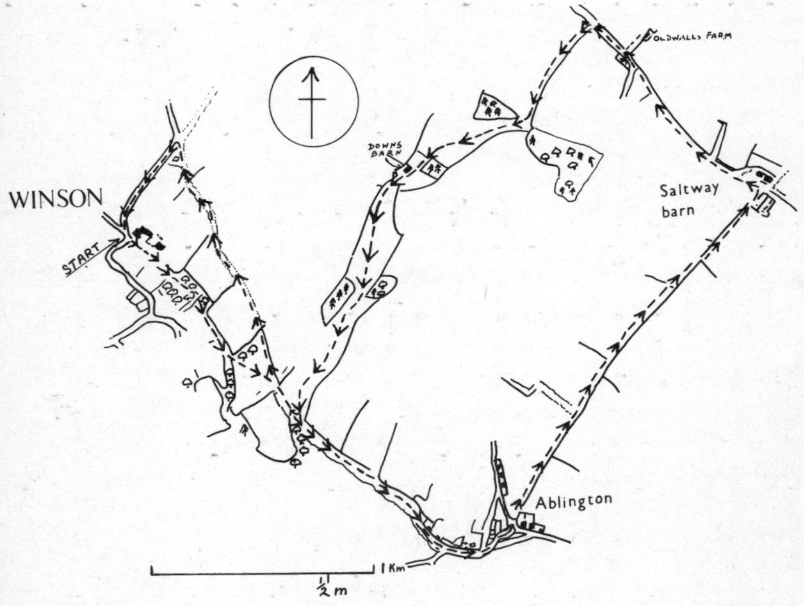

From the bridge walk a few yards along road to the entrance of Winson Mill Farm. (The name of the farm can be seen on the wall beside the two impressive pillars at the entrance.) Pass between the pillars, each of which is surmounted by a heraldic figure, into the private grounds of the farm, and then through an upright ornamental gate into the garden. Follow the stone path ahead past the front of the house itself and past the tennis court to a waymarked stile. Cross into rough shrub and woodland and proceed as indicated to a waymarked post. Continue in the direction of the waymark and leave field over a waymarked stile. Proceed ahead into a wood and follow the definite track passing over a cross track via two gates.

Leave the wood over a stile into pasture and continue in the same direction, SE, with woodland on the right. Near the end of the field locate and pass through a waymarked gate on the right at the edge of the wood and continue along the border of the wood as indicated by the waymark. Pass through a further gate, into a field of pasture and shrubs bearing left to locate and pass through a wide opening in the boundary wall. Proceed ahead across pasture and in a short distance descend to a gate near woodland. Pass through on to a wide track and turn right along the borders of the woodland. Go through gate into next field and continue across the southern end of Ablington Downs with a wall and fence on your left and an avenue of trees.

Pass through field gate to continue along a wide definite track, past a small building on the right and through woodland. After passing through the next gate the walk follows a metalled road with the River Coln on the right and trees on the left. Continue into Ablington and take the minor road, second turn left, past Ablington Manor.* At its junction with the Bibury road, cross straight over and follow the farm track opposite; direction NE. Keep straight ahead, ignoring turns, to continue across open pasture with a boundary hedge on the right. Proceed along the farm track through a double gate into next field and through a further gate into another field with boundary hedge and trees on your right. Continue through a double gate into the next field alongside a boundary fence on the left and then through another gate along a track between fences. Pass into a small rough field partly concreted soon to reach a definite cross track, the Salt-Way, with Saltway Barn seen just ahead.

Turn sharp left, pass through gate and follow the Salt Way, now a minor road, direction NW. Proceed ahead to pass through two more gates to a public road. Continue straight on along the road to pass a cottage on your left and with Oldwalls Farm away on the right. After about 300 yards along the road, turn sharp left through a wide gateway to take a definite farm track along the headland of a field with a wall on the left, direction SW. Pass through a gate into open pasture with a wood on the right. Turn right and descend a wide stone farm track. Go through a gate, past a wood on the left, and then a derelict barn on the right—Downs Barn. Continue ahead through a gate into open pasture and in a short distance turn left and walk down the valley on a definite footpath, direction S.

Pass through another gate into further grassland and keep in the valley to its end at a facing wood. Here make a right hand U turn and take the farm track, with boundary wall on the left, to ascend out of the valley, direction NW. Continue up track and go through gate on to Ablington

Downs and follow the wall on the right to an enclosed lane called Potlicker's Lane. Pass through gate and proceed down the lane with trees and bushes on each side to its end at the road. Turn left down the road and in less than ½ mile the bridge near Winson Mill Farm is reached, the beginning and end of the walk.

*Ablington Manor was once the home of Arthur Gibbs who wrote the well known book 'A Cotswold Village'.

Ramble 10, The River Coln near Bibury

COLN ST. ALDWYN AND BIBURY

An attractive walk linking the Coln Valley villages.
Distance: 5½ miles.
Maps: OS 163 in the 1:50 000 series and SP 00/10 in the 1:25 000 Pathfinder series.
Starting Point: Grid reference 144 047—bridge over the River Coln at Coln St. Aldwyn.
To get to the Starting Point from Northleach take the A429 Cirencester road for 5 miles to the public house at Foss Cross. Turn left and in 5 miles pass through Bibury and continue for a further 2 miles to Coln St. Aldwyn.

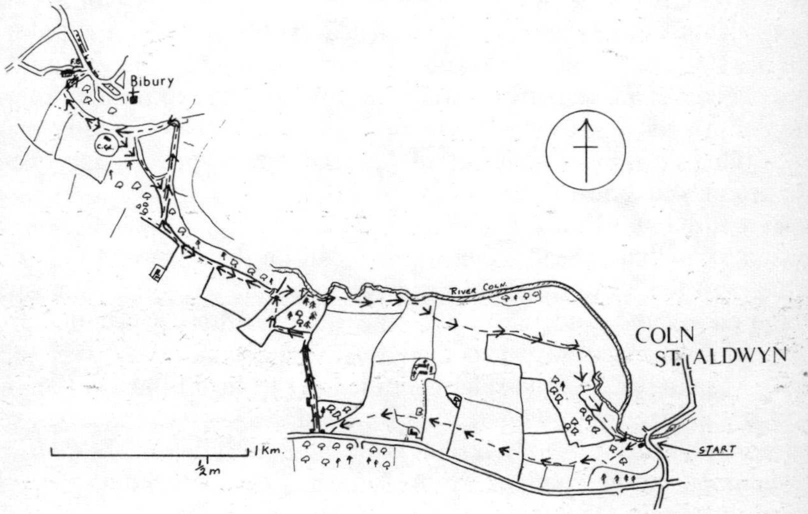

From the bridge leaving Coln St. Aldwyn take the signposted bridleway on the right through the gates and past a cottage and ascend across pasture in the direction indicated. Follow the footpath uphill beneath trees and go through an iron gate to further pasture and parkland in a westerly direction. With a boundary wall on your left follow the definite track alongside to pass through an iron gate into a cultivated field. Continue ahead on a footpath across the cultivation towards a house seen in the distance. Going across the field the footpath bears right to pass through a gateway in the facing boundary wall into another cultivated field. Follow the footpath across and pass through a gate on to a farm road. Cross over and pass to the immediate left of the house towards which the direction had been aimed. Farm buildings can be seen away to the left.

Proceed ahead across pasture and pass into another field through a metal gate. Continue ahead across pasture towards a cottage near the left hand corner of the field, at the end of which locate and pass through a gate on to the road. Turn right, and in about 50 yards turn right again to follow a wide farm track between two cottages—Coneygar Cottages. Continue to where the track forks at Ash Copse, then take the left fork to follow a wide track on the edge of the wood; direction westerly. Pass through a gate into open pasture and descend to a facing wall, bearing right to locate a wicket gate via a small bridge. Pass through into shrubland and follow the definite track ascending to another gate with a Bibury Court Estate notice attached. Pass through and follow the footpath with a wall on the right and a fence on the left and continue along the headland of a cultivated field. Go through another gate where the track becomes a lane between woodland. At a fork keep right to follow the wall round. Pass through a double gate and descend on a wide stone track. Cross another double gate and ascend to a footpath signpost near the grounds of a new Cotswold mansion.

Here turn left on a wide stone track to pass through a double gate into pasture. Continue ahead alongside the wall on the right and follow it round past the Bibury Cricket Field—away on the left—to a stone stile at the end of the field. Cross the stile and pass through woodland to descend on a wide track to another stone stile, signposted. Cross, turn right, soon to reach a footbridge over the river Coln at Bibury. From the bridge walk back towards Arlington Row and in a short distance go over the stone stile on the left. (N.B. This is the same stile crossed a litle earlier in the opposite direction.) Take the indicated track ascending through woodland. Follow the track to the end of the wood and cross a stone stile into pasture and parkland. Proceed ahead alongside a wall on the left and continue past the cricket field (the same one mentioned earlier) on the immediate right towards a wood ahead; direction SE. Make for the corner of the field by the wood to go over a stile and follow a definite track at the edge of the wood with a wire fence on the right.

Pass over a stile into pasture and continue ahead with a wall and the wood on the right. Continue over a stile on to grassland and ascend to pass through a gate; then bear left with a wood on the left. Where the track turns right, keep ahead down a green track; direction SE. Pass through a gate and go along the headland of a cultivated field straight ahead with a boundary wall and a wood on the left. The track descends with a wire fence on the right and a wall on the left to pass through a gate with the

Bibury Court Estate notice attached. Continue downhill and go through a wicket gate and over a small platform bridge into pasture. Bear left, direction east, with Ash copse on the right and continue through a gate and along the edge of a wood on a wide track with the river Coln on the immediate left. Pass through another gate and continue straight ahead across further pasture land down the valley with the river now away on the left. Leave the pasture through a gate and continue along a wide track with a cultivated field on the right and the river on the left.

Follow alongside the river to the end of the cultivated field and at a footpath signpost turn sharp right, direction SE, on a track going towards a wood. Bear left at the wood and follow the track near its border with a cultivated field on the left. Follow the track round to the right to pass through a gateway beside a signpost and into the wood. Proceed through the wood on a wide track to pass through a gate into pasture. Continue ahead across the pasture with a wood on the right and the river on the left, direction SE. Bear left when you get nearer the river and continue through gates to the road at the bridge where the walk started and now ends.

BARNSLEY, round about the AMPNEYS

Distance: 5 miles. Maps: OS 163 in the 1:50 000 series and sheet SP 00/10 in the Pathfinder 1:25 000 series.

Starting Point: Grid reference 077 051 village of Barnsley.

To get to Barnsley from Cirencester leave NE on A429 and continue on A433. Barnsley is 4 miles from Cirencester. Alternatively from Bibury leave SW on A433 with Barnsley 3 miles away.

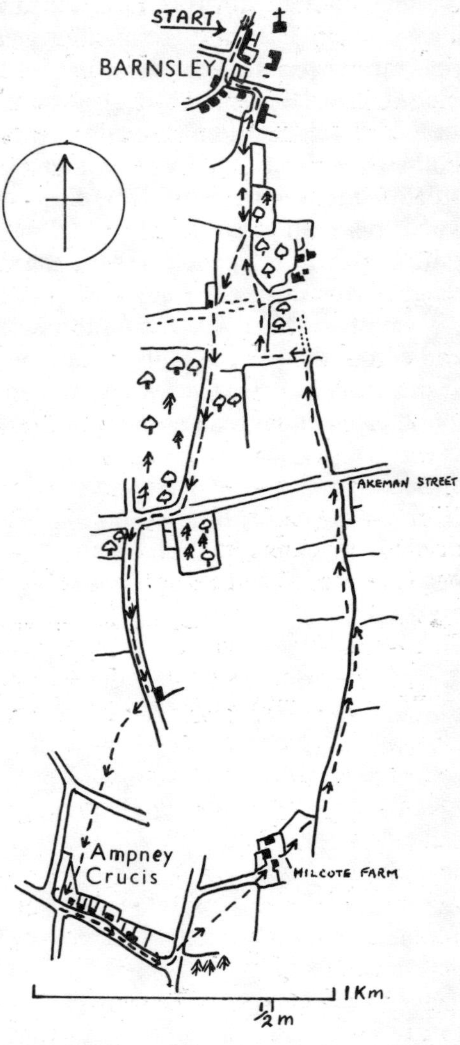

With the Village Pub on the right and the driveway to the church on the left walk down the road for almost 200 yards. Just before Barnsley House, go up a track on the left which runs alongside the house. (The garden of Barnsley House is open to the public on payment of a fee: it also has a commercial nursery which is extensive and well known for its stock of interesting and rare plants. In 1988 the garden achieved the distinction of being given the Garden of the Year award.)

Continue ahead with the wall of the nursery on the right. At the end of the wall and at a junction of tracks turn right and continue along the track for about 150 yards to a double gate. Go through and follow the hedge which is on the left. The track continues alongside a wood to two adjacent stiles. Go over and veer right to the right hand corner of the field towards a wind pump and a house. Go over a stile on to a farm road. Turn right but almost immediately go over a stile on the other side of the road.

Make for the left hand corner of the wood ahead and continue with the wood on the right to the corner where another wood comes in from the left. Go over the stile in the corner and follow a definite green track. On coming out into an open field in about 300 yards follow the hedge and broken wall on the right to the road. Turn right and in about 150 yards go down the road on the left.

In about 600 yards at a corrugated iron barn on the left turn into the field on the right at a concrete post marked 'Public Foot Path', and walk half left across it to the facing hedge. Locate a stone stile between the second and third tree from the right. Go over the stile; cross the lane and over the stile opposite. Proceed in a southerly direction making towards the right hand clump of Scotch pines and some buildings. Pass between cottages on the left and a single house on the right to the road in Ampney Crucis.

Turn left and in about 450 yards at a T junction at Dudley Farm turn left. In about 40 yards go through the gateway on the right where there is a concrete footpath notice; veer left to cross field towards Hilcot Farm, the right one of two buildings seen across the field. At this farm go over the stone stile and on to the road. Continue down the road following it round as it goes to the left. At Shepherds Cottage turn right and go along a narrow track marked with a concrete sign, with a house called Hilcot View on the right.

Go over a stile and on in the same direction across the field for 150 yards and pass over two stiles in the facing hedge at a point about 80 yards from the left hand corner of the field. Turn left and follow the hedge which is on the left over three fields. At the end of the third field go through two hunting gates and over a bridge into the adjoining field. Turn right and follow the hedge which is now on the right. At the end of the second field pass over a plank bridge on to the road.

Turn right for 5 yards and then go over the stile on the left (almost opposite). Go ahead with the hedge on the right. At the end of this field cross stile. Do not go straight on towards a large house ahead, but go over the stile on the left. Follow the hedge on the left and pass over two stiles into the adjoining field. Turn right and follow the hedge on the right to a stile and to a farm road. Cross the road and go over the stile on the other side. Continue ahead with a wood alongside on the right and pass over two adjacent stiles in the facing fence. Go over the next field with the hedge on the right to the double gate passed through earlier in the walk. Now go ahead into Barnsley.

BARNSLEY, ABLINGTON

The charm of this village is a fine beginning to a very good walk—an English village which is simply that—and this is the general character of the walk.

Distance: 6½ miles.

Maps: OS 163 in the 1:50 000 series. SP 00/10 in the 1:25 000 Pathfinder series.

Starting Point: Grid reference 077 051 Barnsley Church

To get to the starting point: As in Ramble 11.

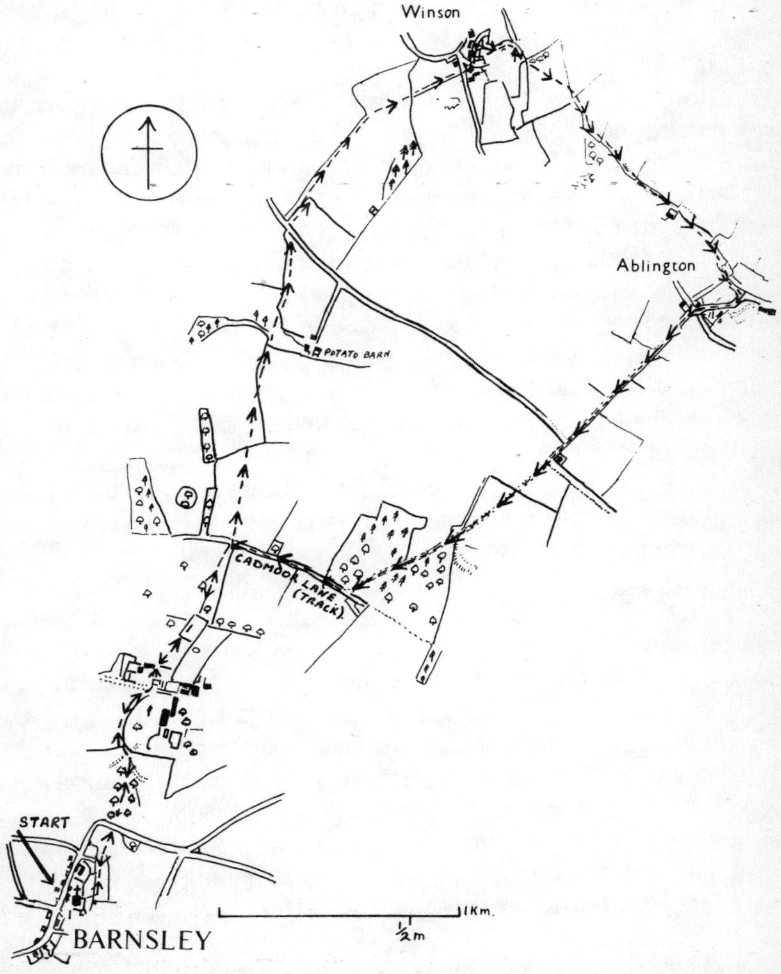

Go through the church graveyard with the church on the right and pass over a stone stile into a small field. Cross the field, turning slightly left to cross the next stile. Immediately turn left and follow the wall which is on the left, passing a stone built cottage and an electricity pylon to a stone stile leading on to the road. Cross the road and the stile immediately opposite, then follow the fence on the left.

On coming to an estate road turn left through a farm gate and, in a few yards, cross another estate road and go through the gate opposite. Immediately turn right and walk alongside a Ha Ha and wire fence which is on the right. Beyond this will be seen Barnsley Park, a large mansion built of stone in the Italian style, erected about 1697. Follow the Ha Ha to another estate road. Turn right through a gateway and, in 30 yards, go through an iron kissing gate on the left, by a drive. This leads to a large, walled kitchen garden.

Just before the kitchen garden, turn right along a path between the kitchen garden and a hedge. At the end of this passage go through a wicket gate and continue ahead with the garden wall on the left and towards a facing fence. Just before the fence go through the gate on the left and turn right. Walk half-right towards a shack with a corrugated iron roof. (The shack does not look very permanent.) In the facing fence, and about 60 yards from the wall on the right, is a stone stile. Cross the stile and go ahead between two lines of widely spaced trees which lead to a wooden gate in a wall. Make for a high stone stile about 60 yards to the left of the gate and cross this into an overgrown lane. This is known as Cadmoor Lane. Cross the lane and through the gap into the next field. (If the gap is heavily overgrown there is a gate about 50 yards to the right.)

Go ahead in the same direction (NNE), walking parallel to the copse on the left. On reaching the facing wall, pass through it at a point about 100 yards from the copse on the left. Go half right and, in about 250 yards, pass through a gateway in the wall on the right. Turn left and follow the wall and trees on the left. Potato Barn will be seen on the right about 200 yards away.

At the end of the field pass through a gap into a small enclosure and cross to go through a second gap a little to the right. Turn left and immediately right to keep the fence or hedge on the right. In about 100 yards move into the field on the right through a convenient crossing point and continue ahead with the fence now on the left as far as the road.

At the road turn left for a few yards, then go through the gateway on the right and follow the hedge on the left for about 600 yards to a little copse where a wall turns sharply to the left. Here bear right (ENE) to a facing hedge and a little to the right of some roofs just visible in the distance. Here there is a definite track; turn left and, in 30 yards, pass over the wooden fence in the gap. Immediately turn right and follow the wall which is on the right. At the end of the wall pass over the stile into the road.

Turn left and then, in a few yards, go right and down a very narrow track between the cottages and on to a lane. In about 80 yards and just before a house on the left with a very pleasant garden, look for a stone Foot-Path marker low down on the right by a white wicket gate. Go through the wicket gate into a small enclosure, leaving by a similar gate into an area of rough grass. The path crosses an almost obscured flat stone bridge and a larger footbridge, then becomes indistinct as it swings left through some young poplars to a line of conifers. Pass through the conifers to an iron gate, but do not go through the gate. Turn right with the conifers on the right and a fence on the left to a wooden gate. Pass through and bear left (SE) up the rise.

Keep to the left of the line of trees seen ahead and then go into the right-hand corner of the field and pass through the waymarked gate. Descend with the wall and then a fence on the right and go through a waymarked gate into a definite track between trees. On coming out of the trees continue ahead with a wall on the left, passing to the left of a building inside a wired enclosure. Go through another gate into a wood, then out of the wood and along a rough road with the river Coln on the right into Ablington.

At the road turn right, cross the bridge, pass the drive to Ablington Manor, and go ahead to a junction of roads with Barnsley signed 3 miles to the left and Winson 1 mile to the right. Go ahead over the road and up the track (Hay Lane). In less than ½ mile, enter the road and go on for about 100 yards when the road makes a sharp left turn at Hay Barn. Here leave the road and go along the track ahead. At a point where part of the track swings to the left, veer to the right to enter the wood through a wicket gate.

Continue ahead along the track inside the wood. On coming into the open carry on ahead for about 450 yards to where there is a gate on the left. In a further 40 yards cross over the high stone stile on the left. This stile was crossed earlier in the walk. (The remainder of the walk now becomes the reverse of what has been described and hopefully, has been walked earlier, but is included here for ease of reference.) Go across the field (SSW) as it rises and at the top of the rise make for the stone stile to the right of the shack seen earlier in the walk. Cross the next field, veering slightly right, and pass to the right of an avenue of trees towards the long low building.

Pass through the gate to the left of this building and go alongside the kitchen garden wall. Go through the iron kissing gate on the service road, turn right and, in 25 yards, pass through the gateway on the left. Follow alongside the Ha Ha on the left to the next service road, continuing past the drive to Barnsley Manor on the left and, in 60 yards go through the gate on the right. Follow the fence on your right, passing over a stone stile on to the road and over the stone stile opposite.

Follow the fence and then the stone wall which are on the right. About 30 yards before the facing wall, go over the stile on the right, cross the small field and over the stile to the church and the start of the walk.

Ramble 13, Bisley: Double lock-up built in 1824.
A pleasant looking building which prisoners must have found pretty comfortless.

Ramble 13

BISLEY, HAWKLEY WOOD, NASHEND, HAYHEDGE LANE

A walk embracing woodland and pasture with wide open views.

Distance: 6 miles.

Maps: OS 163 in the 1:50 000 series and SO 80/90 in the Pathfinder series.

Starting Point: Grid reference 904 059 near Bisley Church.

To get to the starting point from Cheltenham take the B4070 to the Air Balloon public house, then the A417(T) to Birdlip. Turn right then immediately left on to B4070. In about 2½ miles just past the Fostons Ash public house leave the B4070 and bear left on to the minor road. In 200 yards ignore the road to the left and keep straight on through The Camp to Bisley. The starting point is to the right of the road through the village. There is some space for parking in the short road leading to the Bluecoat School by the Parish Church.

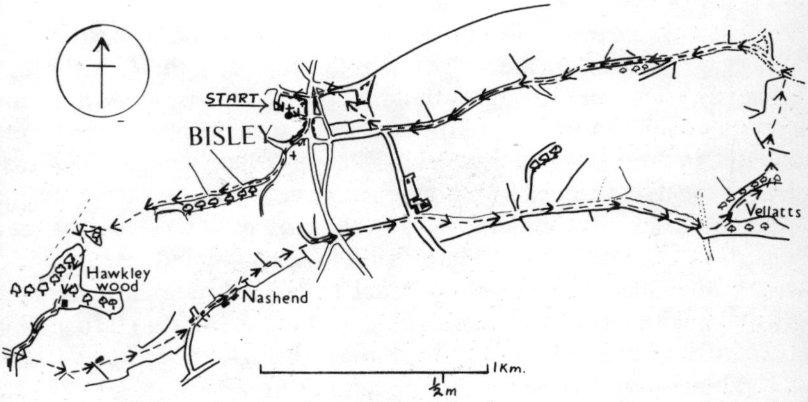

Walk through the Bluecoat School playground into the churchyard and turn left to leave the churchyard by the lych-gate and down to the main road. Turn right, and, in 30 yards, take the right fork down past the very ornate bowl, with seven springs, which is dressed with flowers on Ascension Day. In a further 40 yards turn left downhill on the road signed Unsuitable for Motor Vehicles and, at the next junction, take the right fork on the path up hill. (N.B. NOT the path to Hill House.)

The path narrows as it climbs and curves to the right. Initially the path has a wall on the right and a fence on the left, then walls on both sides as the path becomes narrower and rougher, before emerging on to an open field. Turn left to follow the path close to the wood on the left. In about

150 yards pass through a wicket gate into the next field. In about 250 yards look for a signed footpath leading down to the left. The path is narrow and has posts and rails on the left.

In about 20 yards cross a stile into open ground and bear right and downhill to pass between a solitary tree and a small coppice and on towards the uphill side of a plantation of conifers. Carry on in the same direction towards the power cables and turn left just before them to walk downhill, along the line of the cables to pass through a gate into Hawkley Wood. A rough and narrow track between the trees leads down to farm buildings on the right; the track widens down to Hawkley Cottage on the left. Continue on the path, which now becomes tarmaced, winding up hill to a point where it levels out just before a cottage with a walled garden on the right. About 20 yards short of this wall there is a stone stile with a wooden stile besides it in the hedge on the left.

Cross the stile into the field and immediately aim for the left hand edge of the short line of trees visible on the horizon. As you ascend the field the line of trees will appear to lengthen but the original direction will bring you to a stile by a field gate. Pass over the stile (or through the gate) and turn left to walk with the hedge on the left and out of this field through a wide gap with a broken down building on the left. Beyond this point there are two faint tracks; take the right fork which leads to a very old stone stile in the hedge with a wooden stile immediately beyond it. Cross over into the next field where a house is now visible in the far right hand corner. Walk towards this point but bear right to a gate which will be seen about 200 yards short of the house and in the right hand hedge.

Go through the gate and left on a track between a rough hedge on the right and a wire fence on the left. At the end of the track go through the gate on to a road. Turn left and down to the hamlet of Nashend. There are good views towards Bisley on the left. The road ends at a field gate by two cottages. Continue on through the gate and straight ahead with a wire fence on the right, through a gap in the next hedge and into a second field, still keeping close to the hedge and fence on the right.

At an iron gate, pass through into a rough sunken lane and walk up to the main road (Cheltenham—Stroud). Cross the road and then another one to go through the gate immediately on the right of the house opposite. This is a bridleway and there is a wire fence on the left as far as the next field where the path continues in a straight line, but now has a hedge on the right. The path is well defined towards distant buildings and leads on to a road by a wicket gate and field gate. Cross the road and go through the iron gate opposite with Rectory Farm on the left. Follow the broad green path across an open field. The path passes into a second field and now has a wall and a hedge on the right. Continue straight ahead. In about

150 yards pass through a wooden wicket gate into another field still with the hedge and wall on the right.

Pass through a gap in the next hedge and the track now acquires a hedge on the left as well as the one on the right. In 100 yards it passes through another wicket gate and continues between two rough hedges. Pass over a cross track and continue to another wide cross track. Here turn left downhill. At a facing field gate, with a stile on the left, cross into a field which slopes down into a valley. Cross diagonally left to a gap in the fence next to some jumping rails and downhill to another gate set in the hedge. Cross the stile here and on to a vehicle track of rough stone.

Turn left uphill, passing the entrance to Lower Battlescombe on the left and, further on, a second entrance marked Upper Battlescombe. The road now becomes metalled and is Hayhedge Lane, which eventually merges into a road from Bisley, at a corner. Continue ahead for about 20 yards, then turn right on to a side track which becomes a green track and passes through a kissing gate into a field. Continue ahead and go through another kissing gate on to the road. Turn left down a narrow track between walls and with a cottage on the right and cottage garden on the left. At the road, cross over and slightly to the left, down some steps in a narrow passage and down on to the main street of Bisley. Turn left and almost immediately right up the street to the Bear Inn. Turn left into the starting point of the walk.

Ramble 14, A beautiful by-way in Bisley leading through the lychgate to the Church.

Ramble 14

BISLEY, HIGH WOOD, THE SCRUBS

A varied walk from an interesting village.

Distance: 6 miles.

Maps: OS 163 in the 1:50 000 series and SO 80/90 in the Pathfinder series.

Starting Point: Grid reference 904 059 near the Bear Inn in the village of Bisley.

The description to the starting point is *exactly* the same as in Ramble 13.

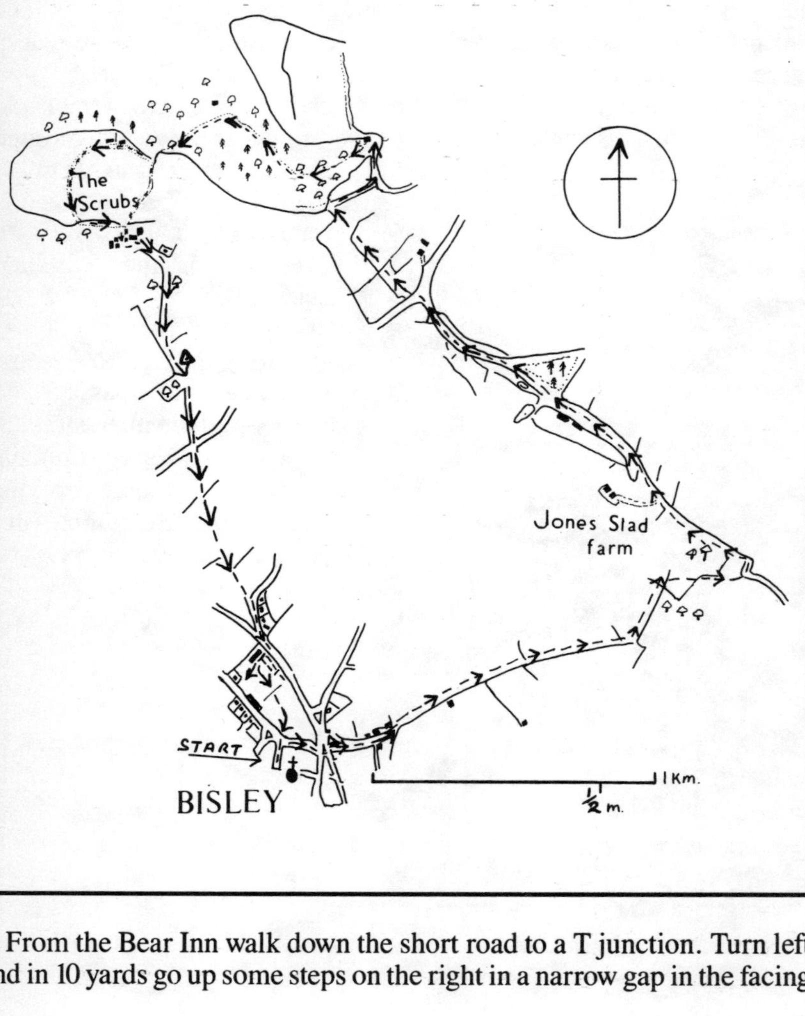

From the Bear Inn walk down the short road to a T junction. Turn left and in 10 yards go up some steps on the right in a narrow gap in the facing wall to a lane. Cross the lane and go up the narrow passage opposite to a road. Walk ahead and continue as it becomes a rough track with a stone wall on the right and a black barn ahead.

Cross an iron stile with a gate on the right and continue with the wall still on the right. Pass through a waymarked gate and descend in the same direction to the bottom of the valley and go through a wicket gate and cross a tiny stream. Go up the slope moving diagonally right to pass through a waymarked gate. Continue ahead with a wall on your left to a green track. (There are farm buildings about 250 yards to the left.) Go right up the track towards some trees and pass through an iron gate on to a road.

Walk ahead and in 50 yards follow it round to the left. Bisley Church spire can be seen across the valley to the left. Pass the entrance to Jones Slad Farm on your left and continue ahead for nearly ½ mile to a minor crossroads. Go ahead and in a further 200 yards another road comes in from the right, signposted Througham. Bear left with buildings on the right, one called Denman's House. The road descends and then rises to the Bisley—Stroud road at a T junction.

Cross the road and go over a signposted stile at the side of a gate and go straight ahead over a field to cross a stone stile. Continue with the hedge on the left to cross another stile. Go straight ahead down the field to a rather awkward stile (as there is a small stone wall immediately beyond) into a lane. Here turn right and in 200 yards, at a T junction, turn left on to a partly metalled track. Continue between rough hedges to a point where there is a junction of tracks and some barns about 30 yards ahead. Turn down the stone track on the left as it descends into High Wood.

In about 750 yards and about 100 yards short of a low building on the right ascend the definite track on your left. At a T junction with another track, turn left and in about 60 yards take a track bearing sharp right. Go over a cross track and continue ahead for a further 20 yards to an open area. Turn right along a definite track to a metalled road with some attractive cottages on the right. Bear left and continue ahead along the metalled road. This road goes round an open area on the left known as The Scrubbs and has some fine views. Walk along this road for about ¾ mile to a T junction with another metalled road. Turn right and enter the grounds of a fine Cotswold house (Sydenhams). Leave the grounds by a gate and ascend to a road, following it as it makes a sharp right hand turn.

Pass a trig point on your left and Stancombe Plantation on the right. At a T junction with a road, cross and enter the field with a signpost. Continue ahead with a wall on the left and at the end of the field pass through a gate and continue with the wall now on the right. At the end of this field go along a narrow path between a wall and a fence emerging on to a road with houses opposite. Turn right and in about 150 yards another road joins from the right. Go ahead with houses now on the right and open fields on the left. After the first block of houses, turn right into Windyridge Road and follow it round to the left. At the end of the road go down a narrow path on the right. At the end of this path cross the road and go down the narrow track opposite between houses. This leads to the parking place at the back of the Bear Inn, from which the walk began.

Ramble 15

CHARLTON POOL, SEVENHAMPTON, BROCKHAMPTON

Woodlands and open country and the pleasant villages of Sevenhampton and Brockhampton and the hamlet of Syreford.

Distance: 8 miles.

Maps: OS 163 Cheltenham and Cirencester in the 1:50 000 series. Sheet 02/12 Stow-on-the-Wold in the Pathfinder 1:25 000 series.

Starting Point: Grid reference 032 237: crossroads about 700 yards south of Charlton Abbots.

There is limited parking for cars on nearby verges.

To get to the starting point from Winchcombe continue towards Cheltenham and at end of the village just past the hospital take the road on the left signposted Brockhampton. Go along the road for about 3 miles. Pass a road on the left signposted Charlton Abbots. In a further 700 yards there is a crossroads. This is the start.

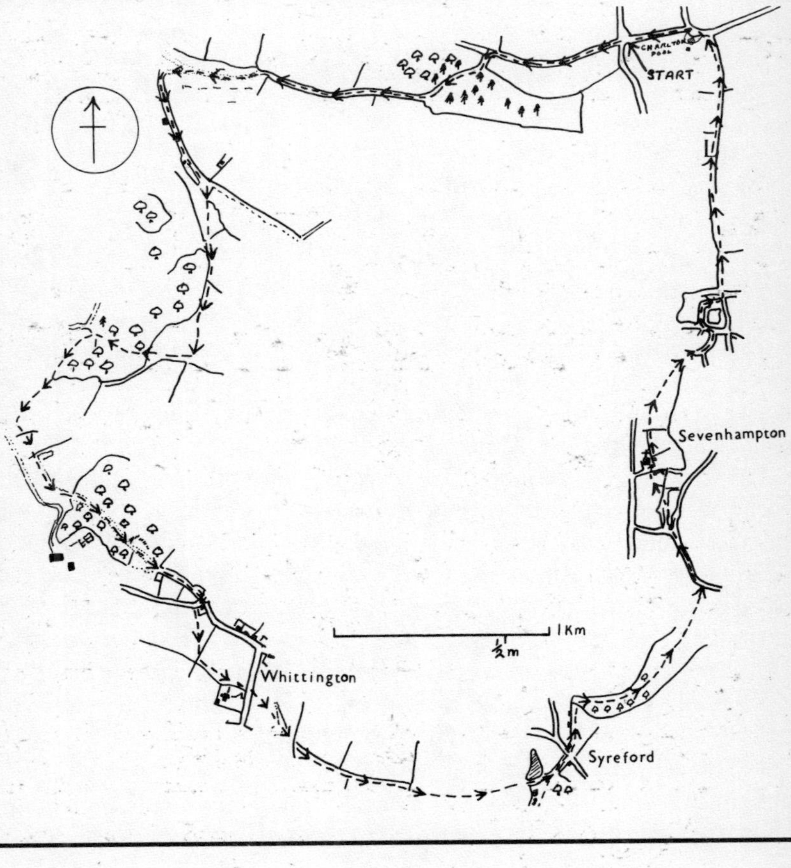

Walk west from cross roads and follow the road to end of first field on the right where two metal gates are found. Take waymarked track on the left. Follow this ascending path through the wood; over cross tracks and along a good path between stone walls. Where the track ends, follow the still clear path through rough pasture for about 400 yards, then take the left hand fork to reach a metalled road after a further 50 yards.

Follow the metalled road passing stone house—Whitehall Cottage—on the right. About 150 yards thereafter pass through the left hand of two metal gates on the right. A clear path is followed for about 300 yards and then aim for the rough high hedge and wood on the right. Follow this hedge and enter the next field through a gate and continue hugging the wood on the right hand side.

Where the wood bends to the right, bear half left to reach, in about 250 yards, a waymarked gate in facing fence. Ignore this gate and turn right with the fence on the left until the wood is reached. Pass through gate into wood and follow the bridle track through the wood. Just before the wood ends, two small tracks are seen on the left. Take the right hand of these tracks which goes just inside the wood. This track could be very muddy in winter.

Leave the wood by a metalled gate and continue on the track which bears left to hold the edge of the hill—do NOT drop down to farm track. You are now parallel to the farm track on the right. Carry on on this track which gradually turns left, passing in front of old quarries and towards a wooden gate which gives access to a wood. Enter, and after two gates, leave the wood to reach a metalled road. Follow this to reach road junction: here turn right. After about 20 yards—just after corner house—pass through wicket gate on the left into a field. Follow the garden wall on the left: at wall end veer slightly right (due south) across field to the field corner and a stile. Cross and hold hedge close on the right. Note Whittington Court, barn and Church on the right.

Leave the field by a wooden gate, cross the road and enter opposite field by kissing gate. Head towards four oak trees in field centre and walk beyond to fence and stile. This field covers the medieval village of Whittington. Cross waymarked stile and follow field path to next hedge and cross another waymarked stile. Hold direction keeping hedge on the left through two fields. Cross definite bridle way track and walk, still in same direction, across descending field to locate a waymarked plank bridge leading to path with Syreford mill pool on the left. In about 30 yards track forks. Take right hand fork alongside building to reach a private drive: here turn left and walk to metalled road: cross and follow track ahead.

Note: On the private drive between Syreford Mill and the metalled road a waymarked footpath branches off to the right. If followed this leads under the old Bourton-on-the-Water/Cheltenham railway track and to the A40 road. Crossing this leads to Andoversford and the Royal Oak public house which offers good food and facilities. This diversion would add about 3 miles to the walk after rejoining at Syreford.

Just before the wood pass between a house and garage and then enter wood. Leave wood by another gate into a field which cross in same direction to a metal gate. Pass through with wall on the left to another gate, down the track and thence to a metalled road and Sevenhampton. At road junction turn left and just before the ford turn right along path signposted to Brockhampton. Follow this path between houses, over stream and stile, up slope, through a gate to reach a field and church seen ahead. Enter Sevenhampton churchyard, and, keeping the church on the left, leave churchyard by a metal kissing gate.

Head towards Brockhampton seen ahead with waymarks on transmission poles. At last pole head slightly right downhill towards stream and gate. Go through and up along path in wild pasture to reach metal road in the village. Pass Craven Arms Inn and at the road junction turn left for 60 yards to locate a passage on the right between houses. This track turns right to reach a road: here turn left and where the road turns sharp right continue ahead into a field. Walk with fence on the left to reach a footbridge. Carry on in the same direction to reach a large tree at the end of the hedge. Here cross into field on the left and continue in the same direction as before but with the hedge now on the right.

After about 500 yards Charlton Pool and the road is reached. Turn left and walk westward along the road for about 450 yards to the cross roads and to where the walk started.

Ramble 16

WINCHCOMBE and SPOONLEY WOOD

A pleasant walk with views of Sudeley Castle and the remains of two Roman Villas.

Distance: 8 miles.

Maps: OS 163 in the 1:50 000 series. Sheet SP 02/12 in the 1:25 000 Pathfinder series.

Starting Point: Grid reference 024 282 Vineyard Street, Winchcombe. Good parking.

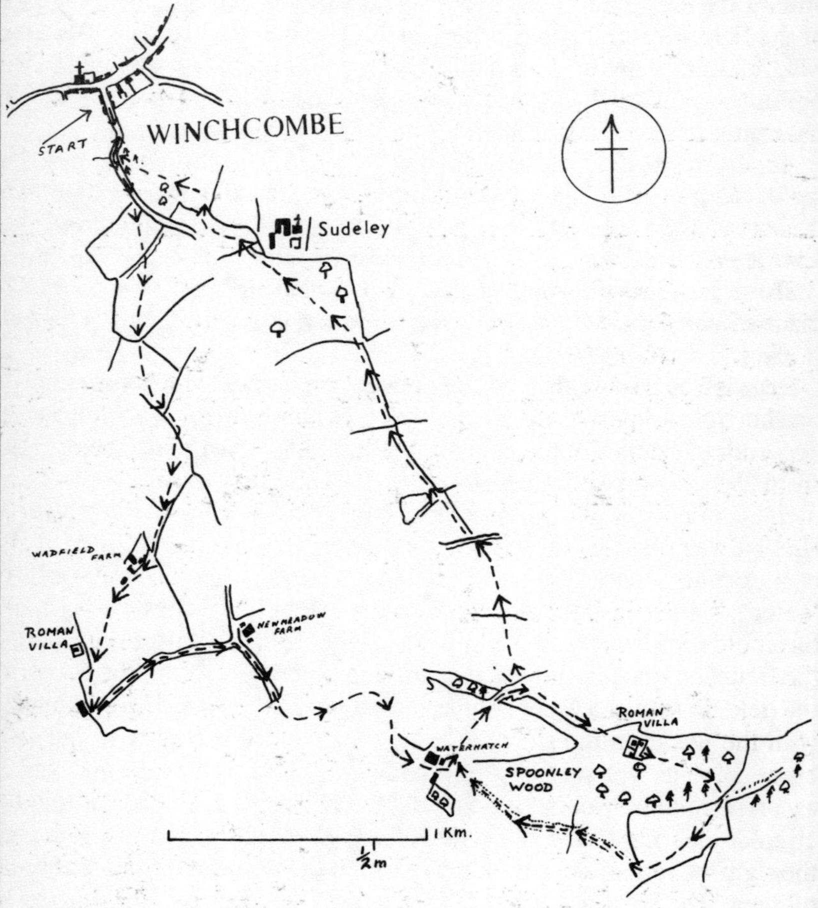

Walk down Vineyard Street away from the town. Cross river bridge and where the gatehouse to Sudeley Castle faces, turn half right along metalled road skirting the castle grounds. At a point where a kissing gate and Cotswold Way sign is seen on the right, cross into the field and ascend diagonally to waymarked stile in hedge; which cross. A well defined consolidated track leads across the field to a white disc on a post. Good views of the castle are seen to the left.

Cross the stile and footbridge and follow another good track across the field to a further stile and footbridge. Cross these and follow track which bears round right hand side of field and which gently ascends. The hedge is on the right and in 200 yards turn right through gap in hedge and over stile. Turn left up hill with hedge and small coppice on left. At the top of the field, turn right with hedge on left to a waymarked stile. Ahead is Wadfield Farm, a fine early 18th century building. Carry on past farm buildings and follow track to cottages seen ahead. These go by the charming name of Humblebee Cottages.

About 200 yards from the cottages, a clump of trees will be seen on the right. This houses, in a small building, a few square yards of well preserved Roman paving. An enlightened owner is to be congratulated on having protected this quite rare example of Roman domestic flooring.

There is no public right of way to the building but visitors are not discouraged provided care is taken. The site is marked on the map as Roman Villa (remains of).

Bear left to pass in front of the cottages on a track which hugs a wood on the right to pass through a metal gate; here turn left to follow the descending track. Although not metalled this is part of a County road from Winchcombe to Andoversford. Pass through a gate to reach the metalled road at Newmeadow Farm. Turn right. The bridleway descends first between hedges then through open fields for some 800 yards, and at a second T junction, turn left and pass between the buildings of Waterhatch Farm. Immediately after the last building locate a waymark on a pole transformer on the left. The right of way follows a route across the field and under a line of transmission poles, to a gap in the corner of the field. Pass over a water course and at the field headland turn right and, with the wood on the right, aim for a white disc waymark at the field corner about 300 yards away. Cross the waymarked stile and follow ascending track through Spoonley Wood. In about 200 yards, a roughly circular clearing is met. Cross this and, in a further 25 yards, locate on the right the remains of a building in which a tessellated Roman floor may be seen. The ruins are about 20 yards from the track but well hidden by trees. The tessellated floor is only about 8 feet by 7 feet and is covered with plastic sacking which has helped to preserve the floor. (It would seem to the authors that even this small area of considerable historic interest would be well worth preserving in a more permanent manner).

Continue along the small, and sometimes indistinct track, to the end of the wood and then ascend, on a broad grassy track, in the same direction, now with conifiers on the right and beech trees on the left. In about 200 yards the track bears right, still uphill, to an iron gate with a waymarked stile alongside. Here turn right along a well defined track for 300 yards to an iron gate; turn right down the track to Waterhatch Farm. Just before the farm buildings, turn right at the waymarked pole transformer and repeat the earlier path across the field and pass over the water course. At the field headland, this time turn left along the headland path.

After 30 yards cross footbridge and stile, and immediately a second stile, and head straight across cultivated field. Cross a further waymarked stile into a narrow wood; over another stile and hold bearing across the next field to the far left corner where a waymark is seen. Here pass through the metal gate and continue along a good farm track. Where the track turns right for Lane's Barn (seen 200 yards on the right), cross the waymarked and signposted fence on the left; turn right with fence now on the right for 200 yards; cross another waymarked stile with hedge now on the right for a further 200 yards to cross a facing track.

Cross the waymarked stile and stone footbridge over a small stream, almost immediately in front, into a pasture field. Sudeley Castle will be seen ahead. Aim to pass the Castle on your immediate right to a kissing gate in facing fence; thence into a small pasture with a children's play area on the right, through an iron gate and on to the road. Turn left and walk over a fine, ornate, stone bridge, erected in 1901, into Vineyard Street and the beginning of the walk.

Ramble 17

SALTERS LANE, HAYLES FRUIT FARM, BECKBURY CAMP, CAMPDEN LANE

A walk with excellent distant views.

Distance: 5 miles.

Maps: 150 and 163 in the 1:50 000 series and SP 02/12 and SP 03/13 in the 1:25 000 Pathfinder series.

Starting Point: Grid reference 048 288 on the Saltway near Little Farmcote.

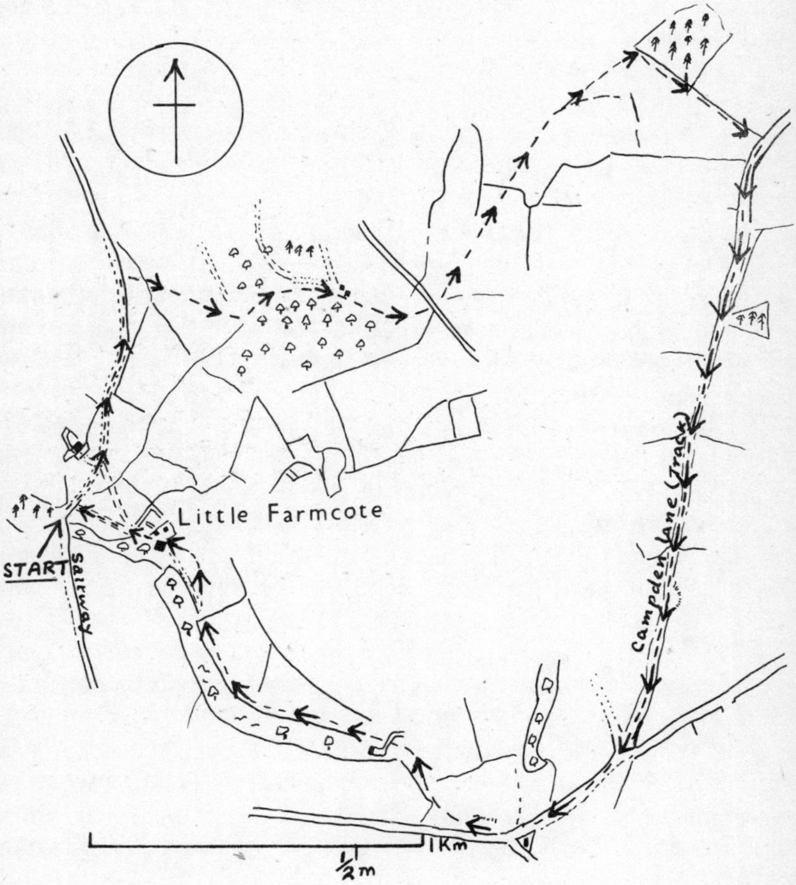

To get to the starting point: From Winchcombe: Go along the B4632 (previously A46) northwards. In about a mile pass under a railway bridge. In a further mile take a road on the right signposted Little Farmcote and Hailes Abbey. In ½ mile at a fork, go right along Salters Lane. In a further ½ mile there is an approach road to Little Farmcote Farm on the left. The walk starts from here. There is ample parking.

Walk down hill for 500 yards to waymarked stile in fence on the right. Go over and cross field in direction indicated to another waymarked stile; cross and immediately turn right through an orchard keeping large thick hedge on the right for about 300 yards to a waymarked post and sign pointing downhill. At the bottom of the hill turn right and in 20 yards turn left to cross a stream. Bear left up hill for 50 yards to waymarked sign; turn left over stream and immediately turn up hill with stream on right for about 100 yards to reach good stone farm track. Walk up track for 150 yards to where it bends left just in front of farm building. Here turn right as indicated on waymarked post into an orchard for 50 yards and then, at another waymarked post, turn left uphill through orchard for 300 yards.

At the top of the orchard bear half left to locate stile in hedge; cross lane and go over stile opposite (direction sign on post Beckbury Camp ½ Km: Stumps Cross 2 Km) into meadow; bear half left to waymarked gate. Go through and continue in same direction through another gate and then towards group of large beech trees, and monument on skyline about 500 yards ahead. Ascend to the monument. There are fine views towards Winchcombe (west) and Evesham and the Malverns (northwest).

Go through gate in direction indicated, keeping close to wall and fence on left passing Beckbury Camp which is on the right. Go through gate and walk towards wood ahead. Turn right with wood now on the left for about 250 yards to gate in wall on the left. Go through and immediately turn right for 80 yards to track. Turn right along this well defined track which is Campden Lane for about 1½ miles.

When the road is reached, go ahead signposted to Winchcombe and Andoversford to where a road marked Unsuitable for Motors comes in from the left. In 25 yards go through waymarked gate on the right into meadow; follow track round to the left to pass to the right of a barn. Go through two gates, 100 yards of scrub woodland and then to a waymarked stile into meadowland. Carry on in the same direction for about ½ mile to Little Farmcote. Pass through farm buildings to join Saltway and the start of the walk.

BOURTON-ON-THE-HILL, SEZINCOTE

A varied walk with, at times, extensive views of typical rolling Cotswold countryside.

Distance: 6½ miles.

Maps: OS 151 and 163 in the 1:50 000 series and SP 02/12 and SP 03/13 in the 1:25 000 Pathfinder series.

Starting Point: Grid reference 170 324 Bourton-on-the-Hill.

To get to starting point from Broadway: Go up Fish Hill on the A44 for about 4 miles to junction with A424. Go left along A44. In just over a mile take the first road right past a garage at the top of the hill. In 300 yards at a signpost on the left the walk begins.

To get to starting point from Moreton-in-Marsh: Take the A44 west to Bourton-on-the-Hill. Pass through the village and take the first road left at the top of the hill and just before a garage. In 300 yards at a signpost the walk begins.

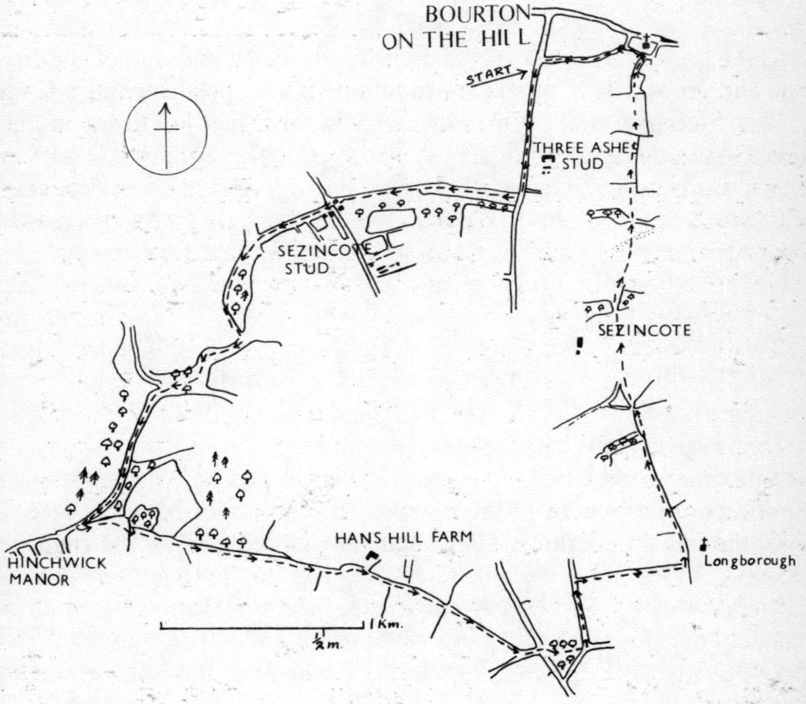

at the top of the hill and just before a garage. In 300 yards at a signpost the walk begins.

Near Sezincote

Walk down the road in the direction of Sezincote and 250 yards beyond the entrance to Three Ashes Stud on the left, locate a footpath signpost on the right. Follow its indicated direction and pass through the gate into field: walk through field in same direction and pass through a waymarked gate into a wood. Follow the signposted track straight ahead through the wood and pass between two cottages—Worcester Lodge and Beehive Lodge—to the road.

Cross the road and go through the signposted gate opposite. Follow the definite track with a house on the left and continue through the wood to leave via a field gate to an open field. Follow the path ahead alongside the wood to reach a field gate at a facing wood. Go through gate and in about 25 yards, at a signpost indicating Hunt Gate, turn sharp right and follow the descending path through the wood. Continue on the winding path to the road. Turn left and walk along the road for nearly ½ mile.

At the bottom of the descent locate a footpath signpost on the left and follow its indicated direction through a field gate into a pasture field. Ascend the field towards power lines,which follow to the last one in the field. At this point swing right to a waymarked stile about 25 yards from a wood on the left (called Mound on the map). Cross the stile and proceed in same direction with the wood—the site of an historic mound—on the left to another waymarked stile.

Follow in same direction shown downhill to the bottom of the valley, through a waymarked gate and ascend the other side of the valley on a wide track. Continue ahead alongside a wood on the left with open outstanding views of the countryside on the right. Follow the path past Hans Hill Farm and continue on a farm track for ½ mile to pass through a wide gate to a minor road.

Turn left along the road to the main road and cross into a small wood via a wicket gate almost opposite. Follow the path through the wood to another road: here turn left in the direction of Sezincote and in about ¼ mile locate a footpath sign on the right. Pass through a gate into the field and walk down the field with hedge and fence on the left and a view of Longborough Church half-right ahead. At the facing boundary go through a waymarked gate on the left (NOT through the facing gate) and follow a wide green track in a northerly direction.

Go through another field gate and past a conifer plantation on the left, through a waymarked gate and then to an estate road which cross to a waymarked kissing gate, alongside a farm gate. Go through and continue ahead across pasture (Sezincote Park). Follow the waymarks into the next field via a stile fence. Away on the left at a higher level is Sezincote House: a tree-embowered lake can be seen on the right.

When Sir Charles Cockerell returned to England after serving with the East India Company he had been strongly impressed by Indian Architecture. He therefore had this house built in the Indian style in 1805. The Prince Regent saw it and was so captivated that in 1812 he rebuilt his new pavilion in Brighton in the same style.

Enter and leave a narrow strip of woodland by waymarked gates to a further park-like pasture. Follow the fence on the right and walk across the pasture to an estate road. Cross and pass through another strip of woodland via waymarked wicket gates. Continue in the same direction past a clump of trees over three more fields via waymarked gates to reach a narrow lane. Bourton-on-the-Hill and its church can be seen ahead.

At the road junction turn left at the minor road and walk uphill. Where the road bends sharp right, carry on ahead up road (marked with No Through Road sign), to pass between houses: then follow the definite track ahead through a strip of woodland. Continue to the road where the walk began.

Ramble 19

SEZINCOTE, LONGBOROUGH, DONNINGTON
An interesting walk amongst attractive Cotswold villages.
Distance: 7 miles.
Maps: OS 151 and 163 in the 1:50 000 series. SP 03/13 and SP 02/12 in the 1:25 000 Pathfinder series.
Starting Point: Grid reference 171 306 near Sezincote.

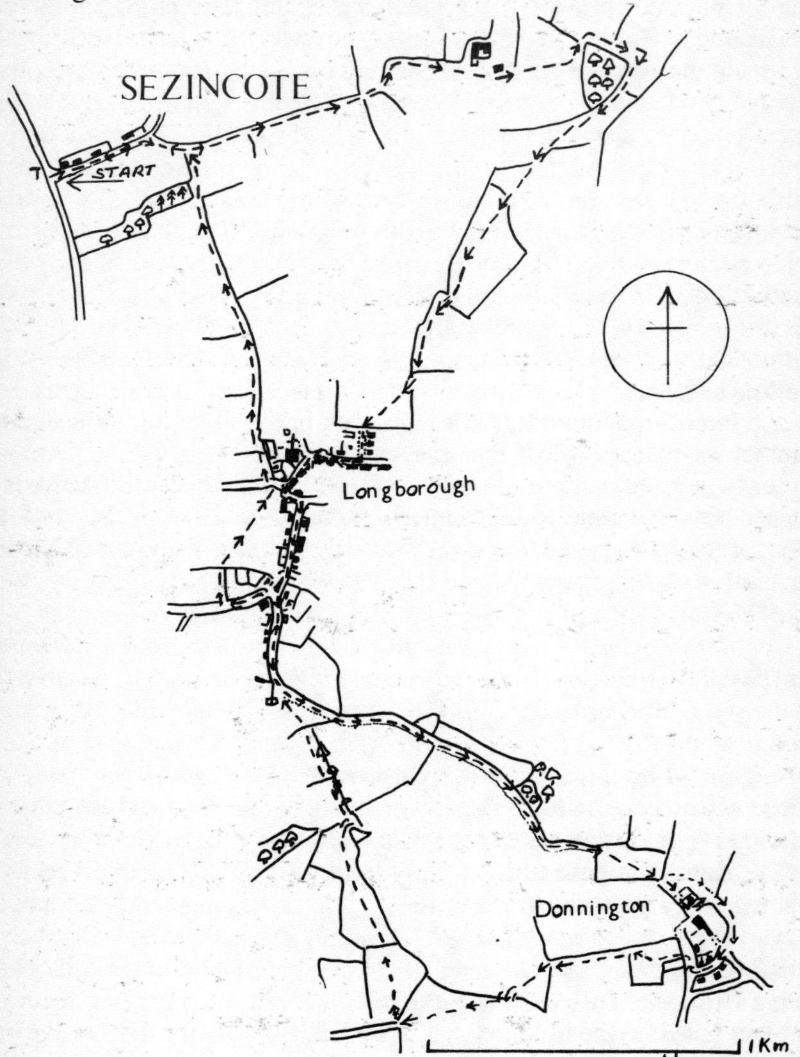

To get to the starting point from Bourton-on-the-Hill in the direction of Broadway, take the first turn left past the Horse and Groom Inn. In 1¼ miles, just beyond a telephone box on the right, the walk begins down a minor road on the left, signposted Longborough and Donnington.

Walk down the road, bearing right and passing a wood on the left, over a cattle grid, to descend on an estate road, going through two gates en route. Continue ahead through another gate and turn left to follow the road round to Upper Rye Farm. Follow the unsurfaced farm-track ahead (ignoring the waymarked gate on the left), past the farm buildings and through another waymarked gate into a pasture. Continue in an easterly direction across the field to the wood ahead. Here turn left along the boundary and follow this round to the right into the next field. Still follow the boundary to the right and continue through a waymarked gate to a hunting gate on the right, at the end of the wood (Thickleather Coppice).

Do NOT go through the hunting gate but bear left across the pasture, aiming for a gap in the line of trees on the facing boundary of the field. Go over a waymarked footbridge into the next field and follow the mark to the next stile and continue as waymarked. At the waymarked gate in the next hedge do NOT go through but turn left and, in 30 yards, turn right over a footbridge into the next field. Walk in the direction indicated to another waymarked stile in the corner of the field. Cross and, in 25 yards, go through a waymarked gate on the right. Cross the stile in the facing fence, onto a tarmac path between gardens, and on to the road in Longborough. Turn right, uphill towards the church. Here turn left, with the church on the right, and go on to the War Memorial. Turn left then take the next turn right, signposted Stow-on-the-Wold.

Continue past the telephone box and, at a fork, descend left. At the next junction follow the road round to the left for a short distance, then round to the right. Proceed ahead down a green lane, through a metal gate by a large stone stile, and down a farm track signposted Donnington. Pass through a waymarked bridle gate into a field and follow the footpath ahead with a fence on the right. Leave this field by a waymarked gate and continue up a narrow green path with trees on the left and a wire fence on the right. The path turns sharply left and ends at a waymarked gate leading into a pasture. Ascend a faint path as indicated and pass under power lines on poles. Walk through another gate towards the farm buildings. In the corner, by a gate, a stile, followed by another one, leads into a farm lane. Turn left and follow the lane round to the right, through another gate into the field in front of Donnington Manor. Follow the ha-ha, or low wall and ditch, in front of the Manor garden, pass through a gate onto a road, and walk up the road into Donnington.

At the T-junction turn right along a minor lane for about 100 yards. By the water pump on the left, set into the hedge, a small gate leads into the field. Walk ahead by the wall on the left until the wall ends, then bear right to the corner of the field. Go through the gate and along the headland of the field with the rough hedge on the right. Cross a waymarked stile into a pasture, turn half-left and walk down the slope to a waymarked footbridge and stile into the next field. Walk up this field, bearing well to the right and diverging slightly from the power lines on the left, aiming towards the trees about 300 yards distant. Pass through a waymarked wicket gate by these trees into a path between two hedges.

Immediately turn right into an open field and bear left across to a footbridge on the far side and about 100 yards from the trees on the right. Cross the bridge into the next field and keep close to the right side to the far corner. Here the path turns right, down a bank, to a footbridge, then immediately left to cross a stile into the next field.

A fine view of Banks Fee house is now seen on the left. Continue across the pasture, with oak trees and a wire fence on the right. Cross a stile into the next field and proceed with the fence now on the left. Cross the next stile and go on to the large stone stile by the metal gate, through which the path led earlier in the walk. Continue up the green lane, onto a tarmac road and again into Longborough.

At the fork, go left, and left again at the cross roads. Walk up the road and, just beyond the entrance sign to the village, turn right at the signposted footpath. Walk across the cultivated field, in the direction indicated, and towards the church which can be seen ahead, following the track to the main road. Turn right and, in a few yards, go left to follow the path signposted Sezincote and Bourton-on-the-Hill. Continue past the churchyard and through a waymarked gate into a field. Follow the path, straight ahead, with a wall and a fence on the right. Pass through a waymarked gate onto a wide track; through two more gates into a pasture, and on to the estate road. Turn left, over the cattle grid, and walk up the road to the junction with the main road where the walk started.

Ramble 20

BOURTON-ON-THE-HILL, BATSFORD

An easy, pleasant walk round about Batsford Park including some excellent views from a ridge above Blockely.

Distance: 3½ miles.

Maps: OS 151 in the 1:50 000 series and SP 03/13 in the 1:25 000 Pathfinder series.

Starting Point: Grid reference 184 343 (right angle bend in road) near Batsford Park.

To get to the starting point from Broadway: Go up Fish Hill on the A44 for about 4 miles to junction with A424. Go left along A44. In just over a mile take the first road on the left, B4479, (this is just before a garage on the right preceding the village of Bourton-on-the-Hill). In about 300 yards leave B4479 by bearing right. In one mile, where the road turns sharp right and descends, is the starting point.

To get to the starting point from Moreton-in-Marsh: Take the A44 west to Bourton-on-the-Hill. Pass through the village and then take the first right B4479. Now follow the description of that from Broadway.

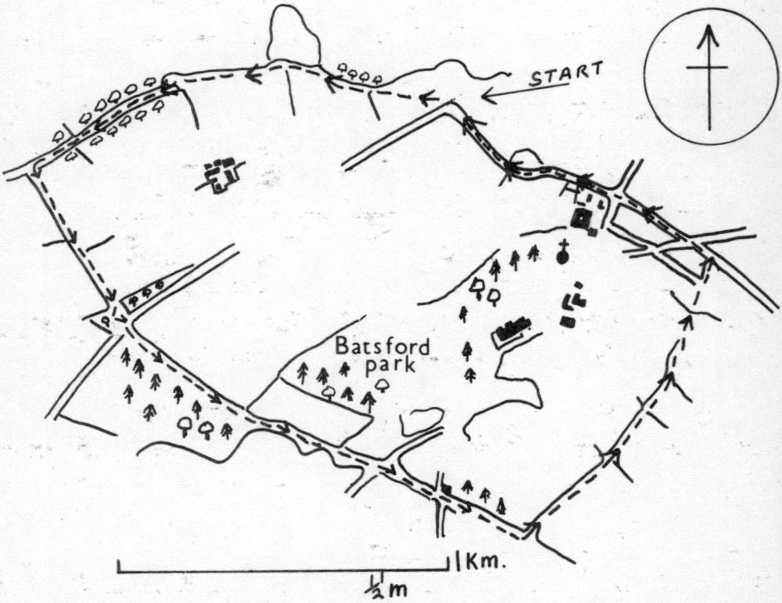

The walk starts from the bridle path signpost at this corner. Walk in the signposted direction—West—across a cultivated field to the facing boundary and follow it round the headland through a waymarked gate to the next field. (It is of interest to notice the thick brushwood outgrowths from the boles of the lime trees bordering the field. Away on the right the views are extensive and outstanding.) Follow the waymarked posts along the headland to the end of the field. Here, turn left for about 10 yards, then pass through a waymarked gate in the boundary wall on the right.

Continue ahead through strip woodland and an avenue of trees for about ½ mile to reach a facing gate. Here, turn left and go through a small waymarked gate in the wall. Follow the field headland with a wall and trees on the right, cross a waymarked stile and continue via a field gate to the road. Cross the road and go down the signposted track opposite via a waymarked gate. Proceed with a wall on the left and a wood on the right. In about 500 yards and at a pair of stone gate posts on the left, turn right for 25 yards, then left along an estate road (waymarked).

In about 400 yards and where the estate road turns left towards a lodge, locate a waymarked post on the right; follow its direction through a waymarked gate into pasture. Proceed with wall on left and leave the field through a waymarked field gate; cross an estate road near a lodge and continue over a pasture field in the direction indicated. Where the boundary wall on the left turns sharp left, go through a waymarked gate (could be very muddy) and follow the headland of a cultivated field in NE direction.

Continue ahead for over ½ mile, following the waymarked gates and stiles, past Batsford Park, away on the left, to reach the road. Turn left up the road for about ½ mile over two crossroads, to arrive back at the start.

Ramble 21

COLD ASTON, GOMS HOLE

Cold Aston has, according to the notice at the beginning of the village, the older name of Aston Blank, both names conveying its high, windswept character. In medieval times it was known as Aston Frigida. The Plough Inn, when visited, was efficient and welcoming—a pleasant place from which to start a walk.

Distance: 6 miles.

Maps: OS 163 in the 1:50 000 series and SP 01/11 in the 1:25 000 Pathfinder series.

Starting Point: Cold Aston, grid reference 129 197 The Plough Inn.

To get to Cold Aston: From Bourton-on-the-Water: Go south along A429 and in 1½ miles take the signposted road on the right.

From Northleach: Go north along the A429 and in about 3½ miles take the signposted road on the left.

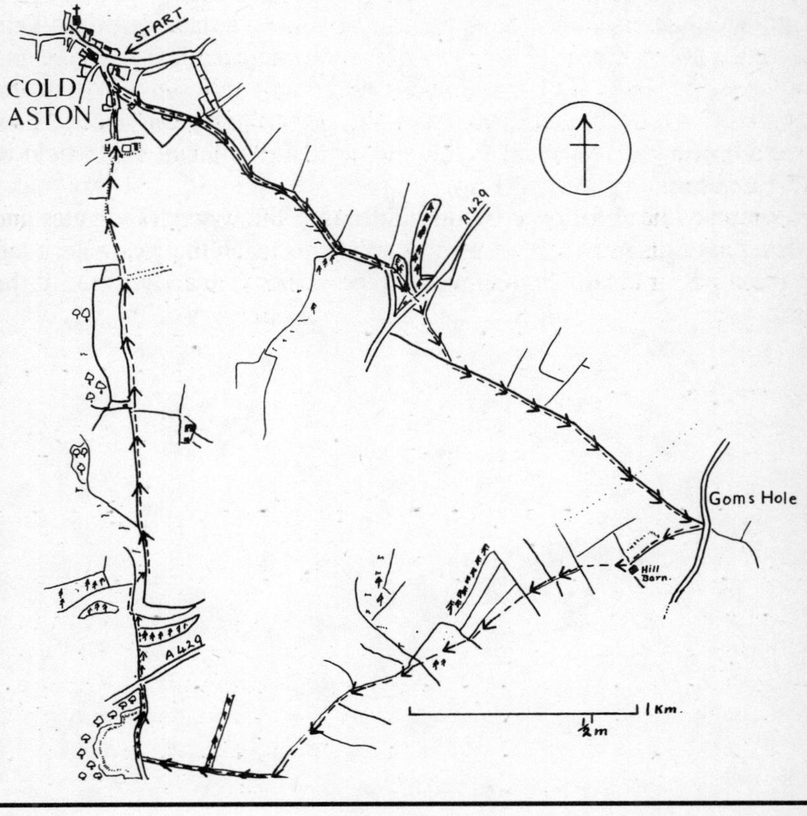

At the junction near the Plough Inn take the right fork going south easterly. In 200 yards, at another fork, go left. Follow this minor road for ¾ mile to a point where there is a strip of woodland on the right. In a further 250 yards, where the road bends right, do NOT go through the gate on the right, but descend a distinct track on the left, through trees, to the main road (A429).

Cross the road and go along the clear track opposite (direction SE) for one mile to a junction of roads and tracks to Goms Hole. Twenty yards before this junction take the footpath which cuts back to the right and follow the hedge on your left to Hill Barn which lies on your left. Pass into the next field and go across it on a clear track half right (due west). Continue into the next field keeping the hedge on the left. Cross the next two fields—300 yards—with the hedge on your immediate left.

In the next field the right of way makes for the right hand corner at the far end of the hedge on your right, but the field is usually oversown and difficult to cross. It may be easier to turn right for 50 yards and then turn left for 250 yards with the hedge on your right. Look out carefully for the beginning of a low stone wall; cross it here and walk half right downhill for 250 yards to a lone tree. Pass through the broad gap beyond and follow the curving hedge on your right uphill through two fields and over two stiles.

When you see a barn and a very clear track running at right angles to your present direction, turn right on the track and walk 600 yards to the minor road. Turn right. At the main road (A429) cross over and pass through hedge by bridleway sign. Descend to valley bottom with hedge on your left. Go through hunting gate and take the ascending path up the other side of the valley to a gate. Pass through and carry on on the definite track, almost due north, via Grove Farm to Cold Aston.

Ramble 22

COLD ASTON, NOTGROVE, FOLLY FARM

A pleasant walk from the same point as in the previous walk No. 21.
Distance: 5½ miles. If a longer walk is wanted this walk could be combined with the previous walk No. 21 to make one of 11½ miles.
Maps: OS 163 in the 1:50 000 series and SP 01/11 and SP 02/12 in the 1:25 000 Pathfinder series.
Starting Point: The Plough Inn, Cold Aston. Grid reference 129 197.

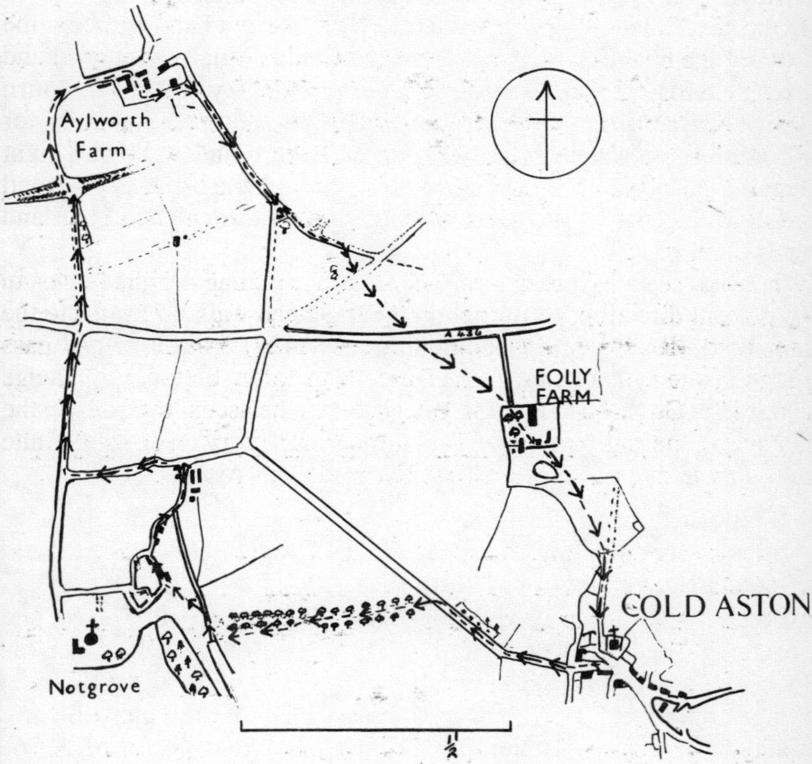

Entering Notgrove

Walk up the road in a westerly direction past the church on the right for less than ½ mile to a group of cottages on the right. About 150 yards past these, turn left thorugh a hunting gate to a bridleway in a narrow avenue of trees. In about 400 yards at the end of this avenue, go through a gate and immediately through a second one and walk along the field headland with a second avenue of trees on the right. (Note: do NOT go through this second avenue although a bridle path doing so appears to be well used—this bridle path is not a right of way.) Go through a field gate and in 40 yards turn right through another gate and along the track for 50 yards before going through a gate on the left and into a pasture field with the village of Notgrove ahead.

Aim half right down the field to locate a gate at the bottom right and thence to the road. Walk up the road past an attractive stone house on the right (see photograph). At the road junction turn right along the road following it round to the left and out of the village. At the T-junction turn left and at the next T-junction turn right to reach the main road. Cross road and proceed ahead into field walking down in the same direction on a grass track with wall on right. At the bottom of the field, pass under bridge of disused railway and carry on down track. (The bank on the right is the site of the medieval village of Aylworth.) At the bottom of the slope the track swings right to pass through a gate and thence to the large complex of Aylworth Farm.

Aylworth Farm, a three storey house of ashlar with a Cotswold stone roof and sash windows was rebuilt in the late 17th century and rebuilt again in the 18th century. One of the large barns has a small reset 15th century window. The farm is named after the Aylworth family who lived there from the 14th to 18th century. One of them took a prominent part with the Parliamentary army in stopping the King's army at Stow-on-the-Wold.

Turn right through farm buildings and right again at the road to the top of the hill. Here the road bears right: the track to take goes straight ahead past buildings which keep on the right. In 250 yards locate a gap in hedge on the right: go through and walk half left down field keeping a small copse about 50 yards on the right and the edge of a plantation seen ahead, as a guide. Cross minor road and, in the same direction, walk first down and then up a cultivated field to locate and cross a stone stile in the wall into the road.

Cross road and go over a waymarked stile opposite to walk over field in direction indicated and towards a clump of trees seen about 300 yards ahead. Pass into grass car park of Folly Court; turn right through farm gate and along farm road between buildings, going left and then right to an iron gate on the left. Take the short grass track immediately on the left of this gate to pass through farm gate into pasture with the wildfowl pens and ponds on the right. At the end of the last pond, bear right to pass through a waymarked gate into pasture field to cross footbridge. Walk up walled track ahead through trees to skirt churchyard and into a lane which leads to the main road and down to the Plough Inn.

BROADWAY, LITTLEWORTH WOOD, SNOWSHILL

A walk with some excellent views.
Distance: 5 miles.
Maps: OS 150 in the 1:50 000 series. Sheet SP 03/13 in the 1:25 000 Pathfinder series.
Starting Point: Grid reference 098 363: small hardstanding opposite Coneygree Lane track by Broadway Old Church.
To get to starting point from Broadway: From the village green on the A44, turn towards Snowshill. Continue past the parish church on the left to the ancient church of St. Eadburgh on the right.

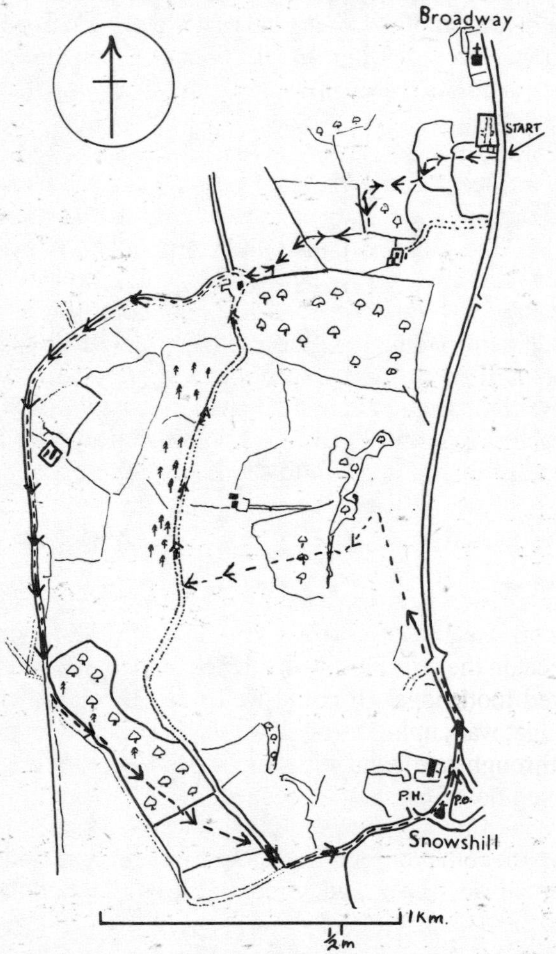

Walk along the road towards Snowshill. Just beyond the cemetery take the stile on the right; down the field with wire fence on the right to the stream and two waymarked stiles; then up the next field to the facing fence. Here turn left with fence on the right for about 150 yards to another stile and hunting gate.

Turn right uphill to a fence and turn left as waymarked and walk with the fence on the right. In 150 yards at facing fence, turn right as waymarked. In about 200 yards go through another gate (or climb stile) and carry on in the same direction with a wood on the left and fence on the right, past farm buildings to the road.

Here turn left through farm gate (or climb stile) and almost immediately go right along track, signposted SHENBERROW HILL: STANTON and COTSWOLD WAY. Follow the clear track, past a clump of fine beech trees, leaving Laverton Hill Barn away on the left and thence to a farm gate. Pass through and in about 500 yards join the road and turn left.

In about 300 yards look out for a concrete footpath marker on the left: take the path indicated downwards through Littleworth Wood for about 300 yards. At a point about 30 yards from where an open field can be seen on the right and the path descends steeply, the track forks. Here take the right hand track to a stone stile and a wooden stile and so into the field.

Cross the field left handed and downhill to a farm gate at road; turn right; at junction turn left and walk into the village of Snowshill, past the church, Snowshill Arms (where excellent refreshments can be obtained) and Snowshill Manor (a National Trust property which is particularly interesting and well worth visiting). Walk on down the hill towards Broadway and in about 200 yards past the National Trust car park on the left, locate a stile on the left at the entrance to the drive to Pipers Grove; cross stile and walk towards three large trees to waymarked stile in facing fence.

Cross and follow directional waymark, half left, downhill across the field to a waymarked stone stile by a large oak tree. Cross and turn sharp left with fence on the left. Follow this fence, and then a stream, downhill to waymarked footbridge. (It could well be very muddy at this point.)

Cross bridge; walk uphill through wood to facing fence: turn right (i.e. do NOT go through gate), and with fence on the left walk uphill and round till waymarked post and stile is reached. Cross stile and with fence on left walk up field to waymarked stile and road. Turn right along road which shortly becomes a good track. There are fine, extensive views to the right; Broadway Tower and Middle Hill House can clearly be seen across the valley.

The track bears left through a gate and leads downhill to farm buildings mentioned at the end of the second paragraph of this narrative. The way back to the starting point is now the reverse of that described at the beginning of the walk.

We hope you have enjoyed this book.

If you would like to receive a list of all Thornhill Press Walking Guides, please write to:

Thornhill Press
24 Moorend Road
Cheltenham
Glos. GL53 0EU